Play the Classical Dutch

Simon Williams

D0813360

First published in the UK by Gambit Publications Ltd 2003

Copyright © Simon Williams 2003

The right of Simon Williams to be identified as the author of this work has been asserted in accordance with the Copyright, Designs and Patents Act 1988.

All rights reserved. This book is sold subject to the condition that it shall not, by way of trade or otherwise, be lent, re-sold, hired out or otherwise circulated in any form of binding or cover other than that in which it is published and without a similar condition including this condition being imposed on the subsequent purchaser.
A copy of the British Library Cataloguing in Publication data is available from the British Library.

ISBN 1 901983 88 9

DISTRIBUTION:
Worldwide (except USA): Central Books Ltd, 99 Wallis Rd, London E9 5LN.
Tel +44 (0)20 8986 4854 Fax +44 (0)20 8533 5821.
E-mail: orders@Centralbooks.com
USA: BHB International, Inc., 302 West North 2nd Street, Seneca, SC 29678, USA.

For all other enquiries (including a full list of all Gambit Chess titles) please contact the publishers, Gambit Publications Ltd, P.O. Box 32640, London W14 0JN.
E-mail: info@gambitbooks.com
Or visit the GAMBIT web site at http://www.gambitbooks.com

Edited by Graham Burgess
Typeset by John Nunn
Printed in Great Britain by The Cromwell Press, Trowbridge, Wilts.

10 9 8 7 6 5 4 3 2 1

Gambit Publications Ltd
Managing Director: GM Murray Chandler
Chess Director: GM John Nunn
Editorial Director: FM Graham Burgess
German Editor: WFM Petra Nunn

Contents

Symbols

+	check	Wcht	world team championship
++	double check	Ech	European championship
#	checkmate	Echt	European team championship
!!	brilliant move	ECC	European Clubs Cup
!	good move	Ct	candidates event
!?	interesting move	IZ	interzonal event
?!	dubious move	Z	zonal event
?	bad move	OL	olympiad
??	blunder	jr	junior event
+−	White is winning	wom	women's event
±	White is much better	rpd	rapidplay game
±	White is slightly better	tt	team tournament
=	equal position	sim	game from simultaneous display
∓	Black is slightly better	corr.	correspondence game
∓	Black is much better	1-0	the game ends in a win for White
−+	Black is winning	½-½	the game ends in a draw
Ch	championship	0-1	the game ends in a win for Black
Cht	team championship	(n)	nth match game
Wch	world championship	(D)	see next diagram

Acknowledgements

I would like to thank my dad and mum for teaching me how to push the pieces, and for all the other help they have given me.

This book is dedicated to the memory of David Illingworth. May his spirit live on.

Bibliography

Books

Winning with the Dutch, Robert Bellin (Batsford 1990)
The Classical Dutch, Robert Bellin (Batsford 1977)
Opening for White according to Kramnik, 1 ♘f3, Alexander Khalifman (Chess Stars 2001)

Electronic

ChessBase 8
Fritz 5.32 analysis module

Introduction

The Classical Dutch is not an opening for the faint-hearted. If you're a player who avoids complications at all costs in the hope of a nice quiet game, don't buy this book. On the other hand, if you're a player who enjoys original positions with a wealth of new and interesting ideas, then this is the book for you.

The Dutch is Black's most aggressive way of meeting 1 d4. White's intentions after 1 d4 are normally steered towards a quiet positional game where White can avoid the complications involved with such openings as the King's Gambit and Sicilian Defence. So what better way of meeting 1 d4 than with 1...f5! ? Playing 1...f5 declares Black's intentions from the start: gain space on the kingside and control the important e4-square. The only way that White can prove anything against the Dutch is to play forcing chess. If White sits back in the hope of gaining a small edge, Black nearly always finds himself in a comfortable position. Tactics based on firm positional principles are paramount in the Classical Dutch, with brilliant kingside attacks against the white king being commonplace.

It has always struck me as strange that so many players like the King's Indian Defence when hardly anyone plays the Classical Dutch, since both openings have many similarities (early aggression towards the white king being the main one). I have always suspected that this is due to fashion – but why follow lines that have been analysed to the brink of death when you can play in a similar sense and only learn a tenth of that which you would have to know playing the King's Indian Defence? Another advantage of this is that normally the black player will have a better understanding and feel for the position compared to the white player. This is due to the Classical Dutch being such a rare guest in tournament practice. I have played the Classical Dutch for about fourteen years and until I undertook this project I didn't appreciate how unique and unexplored the Classical Dutch is. I found in the process of writing this book that many of the positions which I believe are critical to the whole assessment of the Classical Dutch have never been played before. This shows the possibilities available to a player who takes the Classical Dutch to his heart.

History

The Classical Dutch has a vibrant history, having been used by a long line of aggressive, creative and uncompromising players including Morphy, Tartakower, Capablanca, Alekhine, Botvinnik, Bronstein, Larsen, Spassky, Korchnoi and the master of complications Tal. Obviously these players had a lot of faith in the Classical Dutch, and all that remains now is for more players to start testing and playing the Classical Dutch.

The name 'Dutch' possibly originated from Elias Stein, who was born in Holland in 1748. Elias Stein pointed out similarities between the Dutch and the Sicilian. Indeed the principle is similar in that a bishop's pawn is moved to control a central square, and in the Sicilian a lot of Black's play takes place on the queenside, while in the Dutch it takes place on the kingside.

William Steinitz condemned the Dutch after Zukertort played it against him in a title match. Steinitz won the games, and as he had such an influence over the generation of players at the time, people started to distance themselves from the opening. This effect lasted for a long time, too long in my opinion, even though Steinitz played the Dutch himself from time to time.

Alexander Alekhine, one of the all-time greats, employed the Classical Dutch regularly against strong opposition with good effect as the next game shows. Some have described it as Alekhine's 'immortal' game. It combines a lot of important strategic ideas which appear in the Classical Dutch, so is well worth looking over.

Bogoljubow – Alekhine
Hastings 1922

1 d4 f5 2 c4 ♘f6 3 g3 e6 4 ♗g2 ♗b4+ 5 ♗d2 ♗xd2+ 6 ♘xd2 ♘c6 7 ♘gf3 0-0 8 0-0 d6 9 ♕b3 ♔h8 10 ♕c3 e5! *(D)*

Black has played very sensibly in the opening. 10...e5! is an important move, as we shall see later. It gains space in the centre and helps any kingside attack undertaken by Black. Black is already a bit better here.

11 e3

11 dxe5 dxe5 12 ♘xe5?? doesn't work due to 12...♘xe5 13 ♕xe5 ♕xd2, winning a piece.

11...a5 12 b3 ♕e8!

Another typical plan: Black has ideas of playing ...♕h5 followed by ...f4, ...♗h3 and ...♘g4 with a big attack against White's king.

13 a3 ♕h5! 14 h4 ♘g4 15 ♘g5 ♗d7 16 f3 ♘f6 17 f4 e4

White has stopped any immediate attack by Black but he has critically weakened his kingside in the process, and Alekhine beautifully exploits this.

18 ♖fd1 h6 19 ♘h3 d5 20 ♘f1 ♘e7 21 a4 ♘c6 22 ♖d2 ♘b4 23 ♗h1 ♕e8 24 ♖g2 dxc4 25 bxc4 ♗xa4 26 ♘f2 ♗d7 27 ♘d2 b5 28 ♘d1 ♘d3!

Black gives back the pawn in order to suffocate White's pieces.

29 ♖xa5 b4 30 ♖xa8 bxc3!? *(D)*

30...♕xa8 is a simpler win, but Alekhine wanted to create some 'magic' at the board.

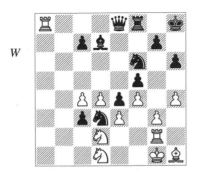

31 ♖xe8 c2 32 ♖xf8+ ♔h7

Black's b-pawn has proved itself to be more than a match for White's rook, which has taken two rooks and a queen!

33 ♘f2 c1♕+ 34 ♘f1 ♘e1

Planning 35...♘f3#. White's pieces are seriously lacking breathing space.

35 ♖h2 ♕xc4 36 ♖b8 ♗b5 37 ♖xb5 ♕xb5 38 g4

The h1-bishop is gasping for air.

38...♘f3+ 39 ♗xf3 exf3 40 gxf5 ♕e2

White is in zugzwang.

41 d5 ♔g8 42 h5 ♔h7 43 e4 ♘xe4 44 ♘xe4 ♕xe4 45 d6 cxd6 46 f6 gxf6 47 ♖d2 ♕e2 48 ♖xe2 fxe2 49 ♔f2 exf1♕+ 50 ♔xf1 ♔g7 51 ♔f2 ♔f7 52 ♔e3 ♔e6 53 ♔e4 d5+ 0-1

Organization of this Book

I have ordered this book so that all classical lines worth playing for Black are looked at. In some cases I have given the reader a choice of two lines, where one is slightly worse for Black but safe while the other is risky but not necessarily worse for Black. The choice of which line to play then depends on Black's temperament.

I believe that is more important for the average player to understand the concepts and ideas behind an opening than the actual moves themselves. I have therefore done my best to explain these concepts, and if the reader understands them and keeps an eye out for them in practice, then he or she should achieve good results. I have aimed my coverage at a wide range of players, from novices who are trying to learn a new opening, to international masters and grandmasters who would like to start playing the Classical Dutch.

Basic Strategic Ideas

The Advance e4 for White and ...e5 for Black

If there is one thing that a Classical Dutch player should remember, it is the following piece of advice:

1) If White can achieve the e4 advance without Black playing ...e5 and Black has to exchange with ...fxe4, White will generally obtain an advantage.

2) If Black can achieve the ...e5 advance he will generally be at least equal.

White normally gains an advantage by playing e4 when Black cannot reply ...e5 for the following reasons:

1) After e4 fxe4, White has at his disposal the half-open e-file, which his rooks can use to exert pressure on Black's weak e6-pawn.

2) After the exchange on e4, Black is left with a passive and cramped position, which is not what a Dutch player is looking for.

If Black achieves ...e5 the position is generally equal for the following reasons:

1) ...e5 combined with Black already having a pawn on f5 gives Black a large centre, and this centre gives him options of starting a kingside attack or holding a spatial advantage in the middle of the board.

2) After ...e5 Black's dormant c8-bishop can enter the game by moving to f5 or g4, or when Black's queen is on h5, to h3. In nearly all cases this gives Black an active game.

There are obviously exceptions to the above rules but in general this is the most important thing to remember when playing the Classical Dutch. One example that normally goes against this rule is when Black has exchanged his dark-squared bishop for a white knight, as the move ...e5 allows White to apply unchallenged pressure with his dark-squared bishop on the a1-h8 diagonal.

The next game shows an example of the above idea that *'if White can achieve the e4 advance without Black playing ...e5 and Black has to exchange with ...fxe4, White will generally obtain an advantage.'*

Ruck – S. Williams
Tallinn jr Ech 1997

1 d4 e6

This move-order stops any early deviations from White, but Black has to be prepared to enter a French Defence after 2 e4 d5, which might not be in everyone's repertoire.

2 ♘f3 f5 3 g3 ♘f6 4 ♗g2 ♗e7 5 c4 0-0 6 0-0 d6 7 ♘c3 a5 8 b3 ♘e4 9 ♗b2 ♗f6?!

White is able to force e4 after this. 9...♘xc3, which is analysed in Line C of Chapter 1, is better.

10 ♕c2 ♘xc3 11 ♗xc3 ♘c6 *(D)*

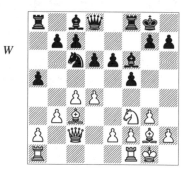

12 e4!

White has achieved the e4 advance and Black can't continue 12...e5?! because 13 dxe5 dxe5 14 exf5 leaves White a safe pawn up. According to the above rule, White should have an advantage.

12...fxe4 13 ♕xe4 ♕e8 14 ♖fe1 ♗d7 15 ♖ac1 ♘d8 16 ♘d2 ♕h5 17 ♕e3

White has a very pleasant position mainly due to Black's lame pawn on e6. It is also very hard to find an active plan for Black.

The next game gives an example of when ...e5 is advantageous to Black, and thereby follows the idea *'if Black can achieve the ...e5 advance he will generally be at least equal.'*

Karayannis – S. Williams
Southend 2000

1 d4 e6 2 ♘f3 f5 3 g3 ♘f6 4 ♗g2 ♗e7 5 c4 0-0 6 0-0 d6 7 ♘c3 a5 8 ♕c2

The right idea: White wants to play e4.

8...♘c6 9 e4?!

White achieves the e4 advance but, following the above rule, Black replies:

9...e5! *(D)*

This move equalizes.

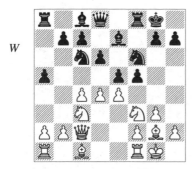

As stated before, this is always the move to look out for. Careful calculation is necessary to make sure White can't win a pawn or that White doesn't have any tactics available. After 9...e5!

Black's pieces become very active: the c8-bishop can enter the game, and the c6-knight has possibilities of moving to d4 or b4 annoying the white queen. Black will get an isolated e-pawn but it is more of a strength than a weakness as it is quite mobile. White also has weaknesses on his light squares, in particular d3, c2 and f3. Play continued:

10 dxe5 dxe5 11 exf5 ♘g4!

This is an important move. White now can't prevent Black from playing ...♗xf5, while on g4 the knight is also a pain for White.

12 ♘d5 ♗xf5

Black is very active.

13 ♘xe7+ ♕xe7

If you compare this position to the one reached in Ruck-Williams, you can see the difference: instead of Black having a passive position where he struggles to find a plan, his pieces are on ideal squares where they put pressure on White's position.

14 ♕b3 ♗e4 15 ♘e1 ♘d4 16 ♕d1 ♗xg2 17 ♔xg2 ♕e6 18 h3 ♘xf2 19 ♖xf2 ♖xf2+ 20 ♔xf2 ♖f8+ 21 ♔g2 ♕f5 22 ♗f4 ♕e4+

Black's plan has been a success.

The moves e4 for White and ...e5 for Black are what most of the opening moves and concepts are based upon. Appreciating these points is fundamental to understanding the Classical Dutch. In my experience, play in the centre is much more relevant and important in the Classical Dutch than a kingside attack, but a kingside attack does appear from time to time...

Black's kingside attack and the ...♛e8-h5 manoeuvre

After move 1 of the Dutch, the pawn-structure indicates that White will have more space on the queenside and Black on the kingside, and so it is no surprise that in many games White plays on the queenside while Black attacks on the kingside. This tendency becomes even more pronounced when White plays d3 rather than d4 and adopts a normal English set-up. Black should remember the following pieces of advice when attacking on the kingside.

1) It is risky to play ...g5 when White can open the centre (typically with the standard e4 break). ...g5 is normally only advisable when the centre is blocked.

2) Black's pieces are on their ideal squares for an attack in the following position:

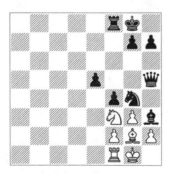

When starting this attack it is obviously worth considering where the white pieces are. For example, if White still has his queen on d1, ...♛h5 is not as effective due to the possibility of White playing e3 and ♘e1, offering the exchange of queens. An exchange

of queens benefits White since Black will find it hard to deliver checkmate without her majesty. An example of Black's ideal attacking set-up is shown in the following game.

Mah – S. Williams
Witley 1999

1 c4 f5 2 ♘c3 ♘f6 3 g3 e6 4 ♗g2 ♗e7 5 d3 0-0 6 ♘f3 d6 7 0-0 ♘c6 8 e4 e5 9 h3 ♛e8!

Aiming for the most aggressive set-up.

10 exf5 ♗xf5 11 d4 ♛h5 12 ♘d5?

This move allows Black to continue with a standard attack.

Much better is 12 ♘h4!, which has yet to be played. Even then, as we shall see in Line C2 of Chapter 10, Black's chances seem no worse.

12...♗xh3 13 dxe5 *(D)*

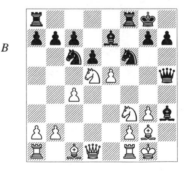

In the game I continued 13...♘g4?! (threatening to win by 14...♗xg2 15 ♔xg2 ♖xf3!) 14 ♘f4 ♖xf4, when 15 gxf4?! dxe5 16 ♛d5+ ♔h8 17 fxe5 ♖f8 gave Black a raging attack. However, 15 ♗xf4! dxe5 16 ♛d5+ ♔h8 17 ♘xe5 may give White an edge. Thus I should have preferred 13...♗xg2! 14 ♔xg2 dxe5 with a strong initiative for Black.

The attack played in this game is an exception to the norm as Black will be very lucky to achieve this sort of attack regularly against good opposition. Still it does happen, and this game shows the potential of Black's pieces if White docsn't play accurately. Manoeuvring the black queen to h5 is a common occurrence in the Classical Dutch and shows an advantage the opening has over the King's Indian Defence and indeed the Leningrad Dutch. In those openings, Black's g6-pawn stops any such queen manoeuvre.

We shall now look at another example of Black using this queen manoeuvre.

Tzend – Knežević
Leningrad tt 1960

1 c4 f5 2 ♘c3 ♘f6 3 d4 e6 4 g3 ♗e7 5 ♗g2 0-0 6 ♘f3 d6 7 0-0 ♕e8

This is one of three sensible moves which Black can choose from. One idea is ...♗d8 followed by ...e5, while another is to place the queen on h5 to exert pressure against White's king.

8 ♕c2

This is basically the right idea since White plans the advance e4. However, this move has a major failing.

8...♕h5 9 e4 e5! *(D)*

The queen on h5 indirectly protects the e5-pawn. This is a good example of following the rule *if Black can achieve the ...e5 advance he will generally be at least equal*. The queen is

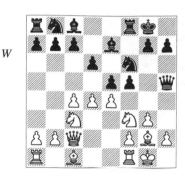

well placed on h5, especially now that White's queen has moved to c2, since moving the f3-knight will not offer an exchange of queens – an option Black must consider when the queen is still on d1.

10 dxe5 dxe5 11 ♘d5

11 ♘xe5? is bad due to 11...fxe4, when White's e5-knight is *en prise* to Black's queen.

11...♘xd5 12 cxd5 ♗d6

Black is at least equal.

13 ♘g5?

This is a big mistake which lands White in a terrible position.

13...f4

Black gains some precious tempi with this natural move.

14 ♘f3 g5

The immediate 14...♗g4 is also good for Black.

15 b3 ♗g4 16 ♕d1 ♗c5 17 ♕c2 ♘d7 18 ♘xe5 ♘xe5 19 ♕xc5 fxg3 20 fxg3 ♖xf1+ 21 ♔xf1 ♗h3 22 ♗xh3 ♕xh3+ 23 ♔e2 ♖f8 24 ♗e3 ♕g2+ 25 ♗f2 ♕f3+ 26 ♔d2 ♕d3+ 0-1

White Plays d5

As well as White achieving the e4 advance, Black also has to watch out for

White playing d5, which gives White control of an important central square. This is not normally dangerous for Black if he can counter with ...e5, achieving one of his strategic goals, but there are times when this is not possible, as the next game shows.

Larsen – Dreyer
Havana OL 1966

1 c4 f5 2 ♘f3 ♘f6 3 g3 e6 4 ♗g2 ♗e7 5 d4 0-0 6 ♘c3 d6 7 0-0 ♘c6?! (D)

This is a common mistake, since after White's reply, Black can't continue with ...e5. The move ...♘c6 is normally only good when White's queen is on c2 or he has doubled c-pawns.

8 d5! ♘e5 9 ♘d4

White now achieves a safe advantage.

9...exd5?

This is another mistake. 9...♘xc4 is better, but White still holds an edge.

10 cxd5 ♘g6 11 ♕c2 ♘e8 12 f4!

This prevents any counterplay. 12 e4? is a mistake since Black can continue with the thematic 12...f4, achieving active play.

12...♗f6 13 ♗e3

White is better: he has more space and a half-open c-file via which he can exert pressure on Black's c7-pawn.

After the d5 advance, Black generally has to keep the equilibrium with the move ...e5. An exception to this is shown next.

Karayannis – Vlahos
Ano Liosia 1996

1 d4 f5 2 ♘f3 ♘f6 3 g3 e6 4 ♗g2 ♗e7 5 0-0 0-0 6 c4 d6 7 ♘c3 ♘e4!

This move is Black's simplest way to achieve equality. We shall examine its consequences in detail in Chapter 3.

8 ♕c2 ♘xc3 9 bxc3

White keeps his queen on c2 so as to speed up the e4 advance, but the doubled c-pawns become a weakness.

9...♘c6! (D)

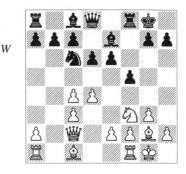

This move, preparing ...e5, is now correct since Black can't allow White to play e4 unhindered. After the critical reply (10 d5) Black's pressure on the c-pawns compensates for his inability to play ...e5.

10 d5

Black must counter 10 e4 by 10...e5 following the golden rule (*if Black can achieve the ...e5 advance he will generally be at least equal*). In this case Black actually holds a small advantage.

10...♘a5 11 dxe6

Other options for White are considered in Chapter 3.

Now Black continued 11...♗xe6?!, which is not best, but should be viable. I recommend instead 11...♘xc4!, when play would probably continue 12 ♘d4 d5 13 ♘xf5 ♗xe6, when Black has full equality.

It is normally the case that when White has doubled c-pawns, the advance d5 is ineffective. This is because White's c4-pawn will find it harder to advance to c5, and so White is left with weak c-pawns for the rest of the game.

Black Plays ...b6

White normally fianchettoes his king's bishop against the Classical Dutch, and there is a good reason for this. The king's fianchetto normally prevents Black from playing ...b6, which is a move he wants to play. In the lines where there is a white bishop on g2, Black's light-squared bishop finds it hard to enter the game unless he can achieve the ...e5 advance. However, if he is able to play ...b6 and ...♗b7, Black develops his bishop and controls some important squares on the a8-h1 diagonal, in particular e4. Therefore if White does not fianchetto, it is nearly always correct for Black to play ...b6

and ...♗b7. The following game, a rare loss by Alekhine, is a good example of this.

Alekhine – Lowcki
St Petersburg 1914

1 d4 e6 2 c4 f5 3 ♘c3 ♘f6 4 e3?!

This continuation makes life easy for Black.

4...b6!

Black grabs the chance to fianchetto his bishop.

5 ♗d3 ♗b7 6 ♘f3 ♗b4

Fighting for control over the important e4-square. Black is already very comfortable here.

7 ♗d2 0-0 8 ♕c2 ♗xc3 9 ♗xc3 ♘e4 10 0-0-0 d5 11 ♘e5 ♘d7 12 ♘xd7 ♕xd7 13 ♗e1 dxc4 14 ♗xc4 ♘d6 15 ♗f1 ♗e4 16 ♕c3 a5 17 f3 ♗d5 18 a3 ♖fb8 19 ♗d3 b5 *(D)*

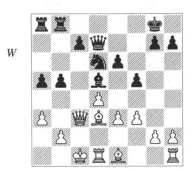

Black pushes on towards White's king, while White prepares to strike in the centre.

20 ♕c2 ♖b6 21 e4 ♖c6 22 ♗c3 ♗c4 23 d5 exd5 24 ♗xc4 ♖xc4 25 b3 ♖c6 26 exd5 ♖c5 27 b4 axb4 28 axb4 ♖c4 29 ♔b2 c5 30 dxc6 ♕xc6 31

♕b3 ♔h8 32 ♖d3 ♕b6 33 ♔b1 ♖c6 34 ♕d5 ♘c4 35 ♖hd1 ♖cc8 36 ♕xf5 ♕a6 37 ♗xg7+ ♔g8 38 ♖1d2 ♘xd2+ 39 ♖xd2 ♕g6 40 ♕xg6 hxg6 41 ♗b2 ♖d8 42 ♖xd8+ ♖xd8 43 ♔c2 ♔f7 44 f4 ♔e6 45 g4 ♖c8+ 46 ♔b3 ♖c4 47 ♗c3 ♖xf4 48 h3 g5 49 ♔c2 ♖f3 50 ♗d2 ♔f6 51 ♗c3+ ♔g6 52 ♗e1 ♖xh3 53 ♔d2 ♖f3 0-1

Black plays ...b5

Black sometimes plays ...b5 to divert White's c4-pawn. After White moves his c-pawn (either with cxb5 or c5), Black gains more control of the light squares, first and foremost d5. This can benefit Black in a number of ways, as d5 is a useful square to plant a black piece. Playing ...b5 also gives Black more control of the queenside. The following game is a good example.

S. Williams – Gleizerov
Isle of Man 2001

1 d4 e6 2 c4 f5 3 ♘f3 ♘f6 4 ♕c2 b6 5 g3 ♗b7 6 ♗g2 ♗b4+ 7 ♘c3 0-0 8 0-0 ♗xc3 9 ♕xc3 d6 10 b4

White should probably try d5 somewhere around here, to be followed by ♘d4.

10...♕e8 11 a4 a6

Preparing the advance ...b5!.

12 ♗b2 ♘bd7 13 a5 ♘e4 14 ♕c2 ♘df6 15 ♘e1 ♖c8 16 ♘d3 b5! *(D)*

Gaining more control of the light squares and the centre.

17 c5 ♗d5

A very good square for the black bishop, bearing down on the kingside and the queenside.

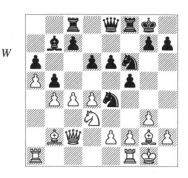

W

18 ♗c1 h6 19 ♘b2 ♘g5 20 f3 ♕g6 21 ♗e3 e5 22 ♔h1 e4 23 f4 ♘e6 24 ♖ac1 ♖fd8 25 ♖fd1 h5 26 ♗f2 h4 27 e3 hxg3 28 ♗xg3 ♔f7 29 ♔g1 ♘g4 30 ♕e2 ♖h8

Black has a big advantage due to the pressure against White's king. I find that one of the most irritating things in chess is playing against your own opening! As this game demonstrated, I did not put up much resistance.

Move-Order

The move-order used to reach the Classical Dutch is especially important compared to other openings since there are so many different routes available to both colours in searching for the position that they are looking for. This is why it is important to be especially vigilant in the opening so you can't get tricked into a position that you are not comfortable with. The only first moves against which I wouldn't recommend playing the Dutch are 1 e4, 1 g4 and possibly 1 ♘c3, and this shows just how many different ways there are of reaching a Classical Dutch position.

Black can use this to his advantage in some cases. For example, if he doesn't have to waste a tempo playing ...e6 and then ...e5, he can play ...e5 in one move. This is normally only a good possibility when White has played c4 and d3 very early on, as otherwise the reply d4 against ...e5 can be annoying for Black, and will not be covered in this book. An example of Black using this move-order to his advantage is shown next.

Costa – Gual
St Cugat 1992

1 c4 f5 2 ♘c3 ♘f6 3 d3?! e5!

Black has already equalized due to his big centre. The position resembles a reserved Closed Sicilian.

4 g3 ♗b4 5 ♗g2 0-0 6 ♘h3 d6 7 0-0 ♗xc3 8 bxc3 ♕e8

The standard plan.

9 f4 e4 10 d4 ♘c6 11 e3 ♘a5 12 c5 ♔h8 13 cxd6 cxd6 *(D)*

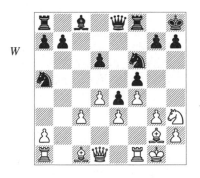

Black's opening has been a clear success.

14 ♕e2 ♗e6 15 ♖e1 ♖c8 16 ♗a3 ♘c4 17 ♗c1 ♘d5 18 ♕c2 ♗d7

Black went on to win from this superior position.

Another way that Black can use the move-order to his advantage is if he knows that his opponent always plays a quiet system that doesn't involve d4. This is normally useful when the tournament is only one game a day, so that Black can check things on his trusty database first.

1...e6
The move-order 1...e6 (followed by 2...f5) instead of 1...f5 has its plus and minus points. It avoids many of the Anti-Dutch systems, thus reducing the amount of theory Black needs to know, but it does give White the opportunity to play 2 e4, transposing to a French Defence. This is obviously OK if your normal repertoire includes the French, but may cause some problems if it doesn't! I've found that about 95% of the time White won't continue 2 e4, but this is a risk that Black has to take. For those who are willing to play the French, I'll just run through some points that are worth bearing in mind.

After 1 d4 e6 2 ♘c3, 2...d5 is a good reply (but not 2...f5? since this allows White to play 3 e4! with a nice position), when White's best move is 3 e4, transposing to a main-line French. Any replies other than 2 ♘c3 and 2 e4 allow Black to reach a Classical Dutch which will be explored in this book.

Part 1: The Ilyin-Zhenevsky System

1 d4 f5 2 c4 e6 3 ♘f3 ♘f6 4 g3 ♗e7 5 ♗g2 0-0 6 0-0 d6 7 ♘c3 *(D)*

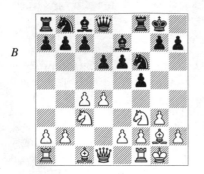

The Ilyin-Zhenevsky is characterized by this position.

By playing 6...d6, Black makes it clear that he intends to continue ...e5. Black's main area of battle is the centre of the board. This can often be combined with kingside play. White's play also lies mainly in the centre of the board. One possibility is to try to force e4 straight away with ♖e1 or ♕c2. The other option is to restrain the advance ...e5 and then aim for e4. This can be done with the prophylactic b3 and ♗b2. Black has many ideas in this variation which have yet to be played, which adds to the intrigue of the line.

The following pieces of advice may be useful for players who wish to adopt

the Ilyin-Zhenevsky System. White's main aim in the Ilyin-Zhenevsky System is to play e4, so it is worth thinking how Black can stop this, or if not stop it, deal adequately with it.

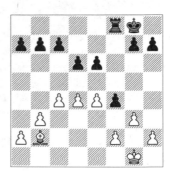

1) Black can in many cases counter White's pawn advance e4 with ...f4. This is especially useful when White has moved his bishop to b2. The move ...f4 will keep the centre closed and generally give Black an initiative on the kingside, while White has an initiative in the centre. Obviously, the pros and cons of such an idea need to be weighed up before Black allows White to play e4.

2) Black can pre-empt White's e4 threat with ...♘e4 *(see following diagram)*. This is normally advantageous for Black for the following reasons:

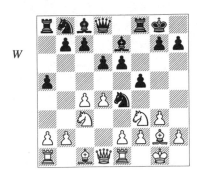

a) It holds up White's plan of playing e4. White will normally have to put pressure on Black's e4-knight with ♕c2, and White's queen may then become a target for Black's other knight after it moves to c6 and then to b4 or d4.

b) Because Black is slightly more cramped than White, an exchange of knights benefits him.

c) The f6-square is available to Black's e7-bishop. On f6 the bishop will help Black play ...e5 and puts pressure on White's d4-pawn.

In the following game I used the above ideas to my advantage.

P. Kemp – S. Williams
British Ch (Millfield) 2000

1 d4 e6 2 c4 f5 3 g3 ♘f6 4 ♗g2 ♗e7 5 ♘f3 0-0 6 0-0 d6 7 ♘c3 a5 8 b3 ♘e4

There is no obvious way that Black can achieve the ...e5 advance, since 8...♘c6? is a mistake due to 9 d5!.

With 8...♘e4 Black makes room for the bishop to move to f6, puts a blocker on e4 and keeps ideas of meeting e4 with ...f4 in mind.

9 ♗b2 (D)

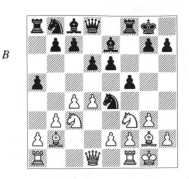

9...♘xc3

White's most obvious plan is to play ♕c2 at some point and then e4, while Black's plan is to meet e4 with ...f4. For these reasons 9...♗f6 is a mistake as Black doesn't have the option of meeting e4 with ...f4 because White can simply reply gxf4, winning a pawn.

10 ♗xc3 ♕e8

When Black meets e4 with ...f4, the black queen wants to be on h5 where it applies extra pressure to White's kingside, especially the f3-square.

11 ♕c2 ♘d7 12 e4 f4! 13 e5 dxe5 14 dxe5 ♕h5 15 ♖ae1?!

Now I played the premature move 15...g5?! and was fortunate to emerge victorious after my opponent missed some chances. Black should first play 15...♘c5. It will be safe to play ...g5 at a later moment as the centre is closed.

There are three sensible ways that Black can play the Ilyin-Zhenevsky System, so this section is divided into the following chapters:

Chapter 1: The Ilyin-Zhenevsky System with 7...a5

Chapter 2: The Ilyin-Zhenevsky System with 7...♕e8

Chapter 3: The Ilyin-Zhenevsky System with 7...♘e4!

Chapter 4: Early Deviations in the Ilyin-Zhenevsky System

Other 7th moves for Black are bad. 7...♘c6?! is a typical mistake; it is normally positional desirable for White to play d5 and ♘d4 (although there are exceptions, such as when White has doubled c-pawns), and this move lets him do so. However, even in this line there are some interesting new ideas. 8 d5! (otherwise Black plays ...e5) and now:

a) 8...♘a5 is an interesting and as yet untried idea. Black wants to play ...e5 while putting pressure on c4. White must play actively to gain any advantage. 9 ♘g5! is best:

a1) 9...e5? 10 ♕a4 c6 (10...b6 11 ♘e6 ♗xe6 12 dxe6 is also much better for White) 11 b4! ♘xc4 12 dxc6 d5 13 cxb7 ♗xb7 14 ♘e6 ♕b6 15 ♘xf8 ♖xf8 16 ♗g5 ±.

a2) 9...♘xc4 10 ♘xe6 transposes to line 'b'.

b) 8...♘e5 (the problem with having the knight here is that Black can no longer play ...e5) 9 ♘d4 ♘xc4 10 ♘xe6 (10 dxe6 is also slightly better for White: 10...c6 11 ♘xf5 ♗xe6 12 ♘xe7+ ♕xe7 13 b3 ♘b6 14 ♗a3 ± Juhasz-Ponyi, Gyongyos 1998) 10...♗xe6 11 dxe6 c6 12 ♕d3 d5 13 ♕xf5 and now:

b1) 13...♘e4?! favours White after the simple 14 ♕h3 (Hausner-Pakosta, Prague 1994), when Black has no play for his lost pawn.

b2) 13...♗b4!? threatens ...♘e4, and White has to tread with care: 14 ♕c2! ± (moving away from the discovered attack and defending the c3-knight) 14...♕e8 15 ♗h3 ♗xc3 16 ♕xc3 (16 bxc3? ♕h5 17 ♗f5 ♘g4 18 ♗xg4 ♕xg4 ∓) 16...♕h5 17 ♔g2 ♘e4 18 ♕e1 ±. White has had to play very accurately to retain his advantage but with two bishops and an extra pawn he must be doing well here. Given a chance he will play f4 and f5.

1 The Ilyin-Zhenevsky System with 7...a5

1 d4 f5 2 c4 e6 3 ♘f3 ♘f6 4 g3 ♗e7 5 ♗g2 0-0 6 0-0 d6 7 ♘c3 a5 (D)

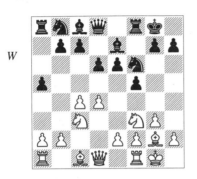

W

This is one of the most complex lines that Black can play, both strategically and tactically, so it suits those who are determined to play for a win even when they have the disadvantage of moving second. 7...a5 is a useful semi-waiting move, as it prevents any queenside advance by White and offers Black a stronghold on b4 for his queen's knight and sometimes the dark-squared bishop. The possibility of playing ...♘b4 at some point is very important for this variation. The ...♘b4 idea crops up at various moments, especially if White moves his queen to c2. A basic example of this can be seen in the sequence 8 ♕c2 ♘c6 9 d5?! ♘b4 10 ♕b3 and now

because Black's knight is defended, he can play 10...e5! with a very comfortable position.

After 7...a5, White has a number of sensible options available to him:

A:	8 ♗g5	19
B:	8 ♕c2	21
C:	8 b3	23
D:	8 ♖e1	27

Other possibilities for White fail to impress:

a) 8 d5?! allows Black to achieve his aim with 8...e5, when he is at least equal.

b) 8 ♘e1?! should also be met by 8...e5, when Black has a comfortable position.

A)

8 ♗g5 (D)

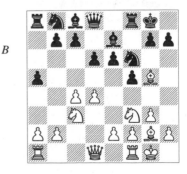

B

White develops his final piece, and intends to capture on f6 and play e4. However, with correct play from Black this shouldn't be worrying.

8...♘bd7 9 ♕c2

White's other options have yet to be tried in practice:

a) 9 ♖e1 (trying to force the e4 advance) 9...♘e4! (this is the best move now that White can't retreat his knight to e1) 10 ♗xe7 ♕xe7 11 ♘xe4 fxe4 12 ♘d2 d5 13 f3! exf3 14 ♘xf3 (if 14 exf3 then 14...♕f6 is fine for Black) and now 14...a4 prevents White from ever playing a4 and therefore threatening the c-pawn. Black can continue with ...♘b6 or even ...b5; the position is about equal.

b) 9 ♗xf6!? (White wishes to continue e4 without worrying about Black swapping bishops with ...♘g4, which we see in the main line) 9...♘xf6 (any other capture allows White to play e4) 10 ♕c2 and now Black has a few options, depending on the sort of position he wants to aim for:

b1) 10...d5 makes sense. A Stonewall set-up is fully justified here since White's dark-squared bishop is no longer around to control the weakened dark squares. White should try the normal plan of a queenside attack.

b2) 10...♘g4!? (the idea is to meet e4 with ...f4, and preserve the Classical nature of the position) 11 e4 f4 12 e5 (12 h3 ♘h6 13 g4 is OK for Black) and now 12...d5 locks up the centre and plans ...c6, ...♗d7, ...♗e8, ...g5 and ...♗g6, while White should probably try a queenside attack with a3 and a later b4 and b5.

b3) 10...♘d7! is a strange-looking move but makes sense: Black wants to play ...♕e8, ...c6 and ...e5 given the chance. 11 e4 (11 ♖fe1 e5 12 dxe5 dxe5 13 ♖ad1 gives Black an easy game) 11...f4 12 e5 dxe5 13 dxe5 ♘c5 14 ♘e4 ♗d7 and Black will continue with ...♕e8, ...♗c6, ...♕h5 and possibly ...g5 with a dynamic position.

9...♘g4!?

The exchange of dark-squared bishops gives Black more room to manoeuvre. By clearing the knight off the f-file, Black also has the idea of meeting e4 with ...f4.

10 ♗xe7 ♕xe7 11 e4 f4! *(D)*

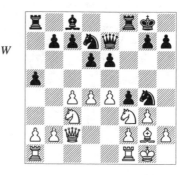

This is a good example of ...f4 being beneficial for Black. He now has a nice advantage on the kingside, and also has the chance to play ...e5 at some point. 12 h3 ♘h6 13 g4 ♘f7 14 e5?! (this is rash, but if White had avoided this move, then Black would have played ...e5 himself) 14...dxe5 15 dxe5 ♘dxe5 16 ♘xe5 ♘xe5 17 ♕e4 ♘g6 18 ♖fd1 e5 and Black is much better, Hartoch-Vaïsser, Brussels 1993. Black still gets ...e5 in, but with an extra pawn!

B)
8 ♕c2 *(D)*

The white queen supports the e4 break but it can also become a target for Black's queen's knight (after the sequence ...♘c6 and ...♘b4).

8...♘c6

This is good now because if White plays the thematic d5, Black can reply ...♘b4 with tempo, followed by ...e5.

9 a3!

This is the best move, preventing Black from ever playing ...♘b4. Moves that allow this knight leap are very risky:

a) 9 d5 ♘b4 10 ♕d1 e5 ∓.

b) 9 e4? (this advance is wrong here, since it allows Black to activate his pieces with the all-important ...e5) 9...e5! 10 dxe5 dxe5 11 exf5 ♘g4! 12 ♘d5 ♗xf5 (a dream position for Black: every piece will soon have a role to play) 13 ♘xe7+ ♕xe7 14 ♕b3 ♗e4 15 ♘e1 ♘d4 16 ♕d1 ♗xg2 17 ♔xg2 ♕e6 18 h3 ♘xf2 19 ♖xf2 ♖xf2+ 20 ♔xf2 ♖f8+ 21 ♔g2 ♕f5 22 ♗f4 ♕e4+ ∓ Karayannis-Williams, Southend 2000.

9...e5 10 dxe5

White's other option is 10 d5, which can be dangerous for Black if he does not stay alert. 10...♘b8 and now:

a) 11 ♘e1 (this move fails to put much pressure on Black's position) 11...♘a6 12 e4 fxe4 13 ♘xe4 ♗f5 14 ♗e3 b6 15 ♘xf6+ ♖xf6 16 ♗e4 ♗xe4 17 ♕xe4 a4 is equal, Petrosian-Simagin, USSR Ch (Moscow) 1947.

b) 11 ♘g5 ♘e8 (this has yet to be tried in practice but seems fine for Black, who needs to defend the f-pawn; 11...c6?! allows White the advantage: 12 ♖d1 ♘e8 13 dxc6 bxc6 14 ♘f3 ♕c7 15 b3 ♘a6 16 ♗b2 ♖b8 17 ♘a4 ♗e6 18 ♗c3 ♗f6 19 ♖ab1 d5 20 cxd5 cxd5 21 ♕d3 ♕d6 22 ♗xe5, Smyslov-Filipowicz, Bath Echt 1973) and now after, e.g., 12 ♘e6 ♗xe6 13 dxe6 ♘c6 14 e3 ♕c8 Black may even be a bit better.

10...dxe5 11 ♖d1 ♕e8 *(D)*

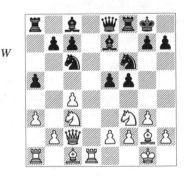

White's pieces obtain good squares in this line but Black has a dynamic centre with his pawns on e5 and f5, so we might expect the position to be close to equal.

White has a choice of two knight thrusts:

B1: 12 ♘b5!?   22
B2: 12 ♘d5   22

B1)

12 ♘b5!?

This interesting idea was thought up by Colin Crouch. White attacks the c7-pawn while keeping the d-file open for his d1-rook.

12...♗d8

12...♕h5?! is a crazy move that doesn't work, but White does have to defend against an all-out attack after 13 ♘xc7 f4 (no stopping now) 14 ♘xa8. Black has some compensation, but not enough for a rook and a pawn!

13 ♗e3 ♖f7!

This move has yet to be tried in practice. Black normally gets his rook chased around by White's minor pieces in this line, i.e. after White plays ♗c5. So to relieve the cramped nature of the position, Black seeks to exchange some pieces with ...♖d7. Black can easily meet ♗c5 with ...b6. Other ideas include ...♘g4 and either ...e4 or ...f4 at the right moment.

Instead, 13...♕h5 14 ♗c5 ♖e8 15 ♖xd8! gives White more than enough compensation for the sacrificed exchange due to his control over the dark squares and space on the queenside, but Black should only be slightly worse; e.g., 15...♖xd8 16 ♘xc7 ♖b8 17 ♖d1 ♗d7 18 ♘d5, Crouch-N.Pert, British Ch (Scarborough) 2001.

14 ♘g5

It is not clear what else White can try, since Black is planning ...♘g4 and ...e4.

14...♖d7 15 ♖xd7 ♗xd7 16 ♖d1

Black can now start kicking White's pieces back: 16...h6 17 ♘f3 ♘g4 18 ♗c1 e4 =.

B2)

12 ♘d5 *(D)*

This is the best square for White's knight.

12...♗d8 13 ♗e3 e4

This is the safest and most solid move. It makes sense to shut out the g2-bishop and gain some space in the centre. Other moves:

a) 13...♕h5 is an interesting but risky alternative. Play could continue 14 ♗c5 ♖e8 15 b4 f4!? (a double-edged way to play, which is probably not sound against correct defence) 16 gxf4 ♗f5 17 ♕b2 ♗e4 18 b5 ♘d4 ±.

b) 13...b6!? is a new idea. It makes sense to stop ♗c5, while Black also has possibilities of ...e4 and ...♗b7. Play might continue 14 ♗g5 ♖a7, getting off the h1-a8 diagonal and defending c7. This interesting position needs practical testing.

14 ♘d4 ♘xd5 15 cxd5 ♘e5 *(D)*

White may have a small edge due to his pressure down the c-file, but his

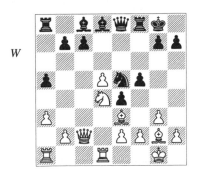

W

d5-pawn could become a liability, and Black has space on the kingside to manoeuvre.

C)

8 b3

This move is a sensible and popular choice.

8...♘e4 (D)

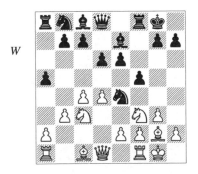

W

As stated before, this is a common plan in this type of position. The exchange of knights eases the cramp in Black's position, and it is now also possible to move the bishop to f6. Another advantage of ...♘e4 is that the f-pawn will be defended after an eventual ...f4.

9 ♗b2

Other options don't promise White any advantage:

a) 9 ♕c2? (the queen only becomes distressed on the a1-h8 diagonal) 9...♘xc3 10 ♕xc3 ♗f6 11 ♗b2 ♘c6 12 ♕d2 e5 13 dxe5 dxe5 14 ♕d5+ ♔h8 15 ♖ad1 ♕e7 16 ♕d2 ♗e6 17 ♕e3 ♗f7 18 h4 ♗h5 gives Black a slight advantage, Maduekwe-S.Williams, Richmond 1995.

b) 9 ♘xe4 fxe4 and then:

b1) 10 ♘d2 (d2 is rarely a good place for the knight after an exchange on e4, as the queen can no longer defend the d-pawn; on e1 it can give extra support to d4 from c2, although in this instance neither square is very effective) 10...d5 =. Black should continue with ...♗f6 and ...c5 given a chance, when he has nothing to fear.

b2) 10 ♘e1 (White's plan is to play f3, aiming for an advantageous pawn-structure; Black should respond actively by hitting d4 to counter White's plan) 10...d5 11 f3?! dxc4 12 bxc4 e5! 13 d5 exf3 14 ♘xf3 ♕e8 15 ♗b2 ♘d7 16 ♔h1 ♕h5 ∓ Hartston-Levy, Praia da Rocha Z 1969.

9...♘xc3!

There are some subtle move-order points that Black has to bear in mind when playing this line. For example, 9...♕e8?! is a mistake:

a) 10 e3?! (failing to take advantage) 10...♘xc3! (not giving White a second chance to capture on e4) 11 ♗xc3 and then:

a1) 11...♘d7 12 ♕e1 a4 13 e4 f4 14 e5 and here:

a11) 14...♕g6? 15 exd6 cxd6 ± Sashikiran-N.Pert, Hastings 2001/2. Black has a thankless defensive task: he is cramped, and must worry about his permanent weakness on e6. The white queen shows its use on e1, as a piece can recapture on e5 instead of a pawn. It is better for White to put a piece on e5 as it keeps the e-file half-open, so as to exert pressure on Black's e6-pawn. It also leaves possibilities for the c3-bishop to come alive after d5; the bishop doesn't have this possibility with a pawn stuck in its way on e5.

a12) 14...d5 is best. Black would prefer his knight to be on b8, but he is still quite solid.

a2) 11...♕h5! is correct. It is better to wait and see where Black should develop his b8-knight. For example, after 12 ♕e1 a4 13 e4 f4 14 e5 d5! Black can continue with ...g5 and ...g4, when he is about equal.

b) 10 ♘xe4 fxe4 11 ♘e1 d5 ±. In this position the black queen belongs on d8, where it pressurizes the d4-pawn. The queen being on e8 makes White's plan of playing f3 far more effective.

10 ♗xc3 ♕e8

10...♘d7?! is slightly inaccurate due to 11 ♕e1 a4 12 e4 f4 13 e5, when Black should play 13...d5 (an important move in this position; if Black recaptures on e5 he is always going to suffer down the e-file). Then Black would prefer his knight to be on b8 rather than d7, since it will be more effective on c6 in this structure. It would also allow the c8-bishop to move to f5 or g4 after an exchange on d5. This is why the text-move (10...♕e8) is considered most accurate.

White has a number of options here:

C1: 11 ♕e1   24
C2: 11 ♖e1   25
C3: 11 ♕d3!?   25
C4: 11 ♕c2   26

Or:

a) 11 e3?! is not very logical, and transposes to note 'a' to Black's 9th move.

b) With 11 a3, White decides to play on the queenside with b4 instead of the centre. However, this plan is not very worrying for Black, who should counter by expanding on the kingside with ...g5.

C1)
11 ♕e1 *(D)*

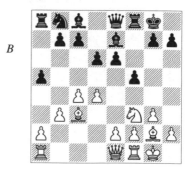

This idea was thought up by the talented Indian player Sashikiran. White wants to gain time by attacking Black's a5-pawn. The other idea is that after a subsequent e4 and e5, White can recapture on e5 with his queen.

11...a4 12 e4 f4

This is Black's main idea against White's e4 push. The reply ...f4 gains space on the kingside and keeps the centre closed.

13 e5 d5! *(D)*

Black can't allow White to open up the e-file with exd6.

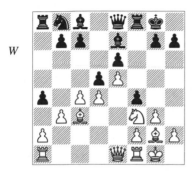

14 ♗d2 g5

The position is unclear but it does not look any worse for Black. Note that White should avoid 15 gxf4? due to 15...g4, when 16 ♘g5 h6 traps the white knight, and it is doubtful that White has enough play for the piece after 17 cxd5.

C2)

11 ♖e1

The idea behind this untried move is to recapture on e5 with the rook, which would be advantageous for White.

11...♕h5 12 e4 f4 13 e5 d5 14 cxd5 exd5 15 ♘d2 ♕f7 16 ♕f3 c6

Black can continue with the plan ...a4, ...♘a6, ...♘c7 and ...♘e6, when his position is fine.

C3)

11 ♕d3!? *(D)*

This untried move brings the queen to its most centralized and natural

square, and gives extra protection to f3, which is often useful. It is hard for Black to find a way to exploit the queen being on d3.

11...♕h5

11...♘d7?! is an error due to 12 e4 f4 13 e5 dxe5 14 ♘xe5! (this shows why the queen is useful on d3, as now Black can't block in the white bishop with ...f3) 14...♘xe5 15 dxe5 ♕h5 16 ♗f3 and White is slightly better, since the exchange of knights has helped his position.

12 e4 f4 13 e5 d5 14 ♗d2 g5 15 gxf4 gxf4 *(D)*

White has a nice lead in development but Black's position is solid; he has the choice between putting his queen's bishop on the a8-h1 diagonal by ...♗d7-c6, or bringing it around to the kingside via e8. Overall, White probably has a small edge, but practical examples are needed.

C4)

11 ♕c2

This has been White's most popular choice, but it is not necessarily the best.

11...♘d7

Other moves give White the advantage. For example, 11...♕h5?! (this would be a novelty) 12 e4 f4 13 e5 d5 is mistaken since from c2 White's queen exerts pressure on c7. Then:

a1) 14 cxd5?! exd5 15 ♗d2 c6!? 16 ♗xf4? (after 16 gxf4 ♗h3 17 ♘e1 ♘d7 with the idea of playing ...♖f5, ...♘f8 followed by ...♘e6 or ...♘g6, Black is doing OK) 16...g5 17 ♗xg5 ♗xg5 18 ♘xg5 ♕xg5 ∓.

a2) 14 ♗d2! fxg3 (not 14...g5? 15 gxf4 gxf4 16 cxd5 exd5 17 ♕xc7 ♘c6 18 ♖fc1! ±) leaves White with more space but the position is still not wholly clear. Play might continue 15 fxg3 c6 (unfortunately 15...♘c6?! runs into 16 cxd5 exd5 17 ♘g5!), when White holds a small edge due to his better development and space advantage.

12 e4 f4 13 e5

This is the most critical continuation, but there is something to be said for the untried 13 ♖ae1. White wants to play e5 and recapture on that square with a piece, instead of the d-pawn. Black has three decent ways of replying, with the choice between them mainly depending on his style:

a) 13...c6 is a safe way of playing, but is not very testing. 14 e5 d5 gives White a small advantage due to his better developed pieces.

b) 13...♕h5 is probably better than line 'a' since it leaves more options available to Black. 14 e5 d5 will lead to an interesting struggle.

c) 13...e5!? has an interesting pawn sacrifice in mind:

c1) 14 dxe5 ♘xe5 is fine for Black: 15 ♘xe5 (15 ♗xe5 dxe5 16 ♘xe5 ♗b4 is good for Black) 15...dxe5 16 ♗xe5 f3 17 ♗h1 ♗h3 and Black wins the exchange.

c2) 14 gxf4 ♖xf4 15 dxe5 ♕g6 16 ♔h1 (16 exd6 ♗xd6) 16...♘c5 gives Black compensation for the pawn, but whether it is enough is yet to be seen.

13...dxe5 14 dxe5 ♕h5 (D)

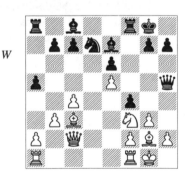

15 h3!

If White doesn't play h3 he has to watch out for ...g5-g4. 15 ♖ae1?! is best met by 15...♘c5 with ideas of playing ...g5 in the near future. This is better than 15...g5?! 16 ♘d2 f3 17 ♘xf3 ♖xf3 18 ♕d1 g4 19 ♗xf3 gxf3 20 ♖e3 ♕g6 21 ♕xf3 ♘c5 22 ♗d4 ♗d7 23 ♗xc5 ♗xc5 24 ♕xb7 ♕e8 25

♖e4?? (25 ♖d3 ±) 25...♗c6 26 ♖g4+ ♔h8 27 ♕xc7 ♖a7 0-1 Kemp-S.Williams, British Ch (Millfield) 2000.

15...♘c5 16 g4 ♕h6

Khalifman believes that White is better in this position. This may be true, but any advantage is marginal.

17 ♔h2!

With this move White is trying to consolidate his kingside. Other options aren't convincing; for example, 17 a3?! is the wrong plan: 17...♗d7 18 b4 ♘a4 19 ♗d2 ♗c6 20 ♔h2 ♖ad8 (Black's pieces are the more active, and White's queenside pawns and airy kingside could prove a liability) 21 ♖ad1 axb4 22 axb4 ♘b6 23 b5 ♗xf3 24 ♗xf3 ♖d4 and Black has a slight advantage, Beaumont-S.Williams, British League (4NCL) 2001/2.

17...♗d7 18 ♘d4

Black has two options now, one of which is a bit suspect but requires accurate play from White, while the other gives White a small edge without much risk.

18...♗e8

This untried idea leads to an unbalanced position where White's chances may be fractionally better. This is safer than 18...f3?!, which is tricky for White to handle but it is not entirely sound: 19 ♘xf3 (19 ♗d2? ♗g5 ∓; 19 ♗xf3? ♖xf3 20 ♘xf3 ♕f4+ 21 ♔g2 ♗c6 22 ♕e2 ♖f8 is also slightly better for Black) 19...♕f4+ 20 ♔g1 ♗c6, and now:

a) 21 ♗d2?! allows Black to play a queen good sacrifice: 21...♕xf3! 22 ♗xf3 ♖xf3 23 ♔h2 ♘d3, Vigus-S.Williams, Witley 2000. Black has ample

compensation: the c6-bishop is a monster, while he has the open f-file and an active knight. White did well to survive in the game.

b) 21 ♘h2! ± is best. Black has some play for the pawn but it is doubtful whether it is enough.

19 ♕e2 ♗g6 20 ♖fd1 c6 (D)

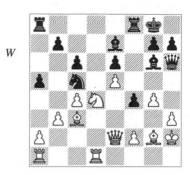

This position is murky, but possibly White holds a slight edge due to his more centralized pieces. He can also try to expand on the queenside at some point with a3 and b4. Black should probably play ...♖ad8 with the idea of sacrificing a pawn with ...f3 at the correct moment. This should be combined with dropping a piece into d3.

D)

8 ♖e1

This is the most forcing and critical continuation.

8...♘e4 (D)

Blocking White's e4 break. Other moves allow e4, when White is clearly better.

9 ♕c2

This natural move forces Black to decide what he is going to do with his

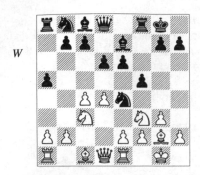

W

knight, and is the only way White can attempt to achieve an advantage. Other moves:

a) 9 ♘xe4 is a rare move that gives Black time to achieve active counterplay: 9...fxe4 10 ♘d2 d5 11 f3 (now if White could have everything his own way he would slowly control and exploit the e5-square, but Black never sits still in the Dutch) 11...exf3 12 ♘xf3 c5 13 ♗e3 (this is an improvement over 13 cxd5 exd5 14 ♗e3 c4, when Black is clearly better due to his mobile queenside pawn-mass) 13...cxd4 14 ♘xd4 dxc4 ∓. Black stands well here; if he can play ...e5 all his pieces will spring to life.

b) 9 ♕d3 usually transposes to Line D1, but there are some other options for both sides:

b1) 9...d5!? aims for a Stonewall set-up. This is justified here, as White's pieces are misplaced. The white knight normally goes to d3 in the Stonewall but it would take a long time to manoeuvre it around to this square here. However, the ...d5 set-up may not appeal to all Classical Dutch enthusiasts.

b2) 9...♘xc3 10 bxc3 (10 ♕xc3 transposes to Line D1) 10...♘c6! 11

d5 ♘e5 12 ♘xe5 (12 ♕d4 ♘xf3+ 13 exf3 e5 ∓ and Black plays ...f4! next move; otherwise, White would play f4 himself, gaining a small advantage) 12...dxe5 =.

9...♘xc3!

The old main line is 9...♘c6?! but it has been refuted now: 10 ♘xe4 ♘b4 11 ♕b1 fxe4 12 ♕xe4 e5 13 dxe5! (13 g4? used to be played regularly but Black has a couple of ways to achieve satisfactory play for his pawn; for example, 13...c6 14 a3 d5 15 cxd5 cxd5 16 ♕b1 e4) 13...♗f5 14 ♕xb7 ♖b8 15 ♕a7 ±.

Now:

D1: 10 ♕xc3   28
D2: 10 bxc3   30

Both these moves have their pluses and minuses.

D1)
10 ♕xc3

This is the most principled move. White wishes to keep his c-pawns intact and play e4, when he would have the advantage. Black must stop White having everything his own way, and play can now get very complicated.

10...♘c6 11 e4 (D)

Other moves don't trouble Black; for example, 11 d5 ♗f6 12 ♕d2 ♘e7 13 ♘d4 e5 14 ♘b5 ∓ Pigusov-Atalik, Beijing 1997.

11...e5!

This is the only way to deny White an edge. For example:

a) 11...fxe4? 12 ♖xe4 ± gives White just the kind of position he is looking for, with more space, pressure on e6 and an easy plan of development.

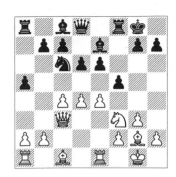

B

b) 11...d5? is another mistake that Black has committed far too often. 12 exd5 ♗b4 13 ♕d3 exd5 14 ♗g5 ♘e7 15 c5? (15 ♖e5! +−) 15...♗xe1 16 ♖xe1 ♖e8 17 ♕e2 ♔f8 18 ♘e5 ♖a6? (18...♗e6) 19 ♕h5 +− Shashin-Korzin, USSR Cht 1966.

12 exf5

There have only been two examples of 11...e5. One continued 12 d5?!, but it is nearly always a mistake for White to close the position since Black's centre will be rock-solid for the rest of the game. After 12...♘b4 13 a3 fxe4 14 ♖xe4 ♗f5 15 ♖e2 Black continued 15...♕d7?! in Bukal-J.Littlewood, Arco seniors Wch 2001. Better is 15...♘d3 16 ♗e3 ♕e8 ∓, when Black plans to transfer his queen to g6, where it controls d3 and e4.

12...♗xf5 13 dxe5!

This move is an improvement over 13 ♗e3?, which gives Black an easy game: 13...♗e4 14 ♘d2 ♗xg2 15 ♔xg2 d5! ∓ Gallagher-S.Williams, Isle of Man 2001.

13...dxe5 14 c5!

This is the most testing move. Both players must now proceed with extreme caution.

14...♗f6! *(D)*

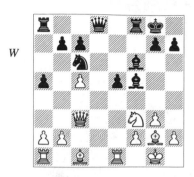

W

The position becomes very complicated after this move, but Black is OK in all the ensuing lines.

15 ♕b3+

If White doesn't grab the b7-pawn, Black has nothing to worry about, thanks to his active pieces. For example, 15 g4 e4 is fine for Black.

15...♔h8 16 ♕xb7 ♘b4!

Black has to play actively.

17 ♘xe5

The complications start.

17...♘c2 18 ♗f4!

Other moves are worse:

a) 18 ♕xa8? ♕xa8 19 ♗xa8 ♘xe1 (White has too many pieces *en prise*) 20 ♗g5 ♘c2! ∓.

b) 18 ♗g5? ♘xe1 19 ♖xe1 ♖b8 20 ♘c6 ♖xb7 21 ♘xd8 ♗xd8 22 ♗xd8 ♖xb2 ∓.

c) 18 ♘c6 ♕c8 19 ♕xc8 ♖axc8 ∓.

Now Black's choice of move depends on his style:

18...g5!? *(D)*

Black's other option is the less complicated 18...♖b8, after which play might continue 19 ♖ad1 ♕xd1! 20 ♖xd1 ♖xb7 21 ♗xb7 g5! 22 ♘d7

♗xd7 23 ♖xd7 gxf4 24 ♗e4 ♘b4 25 ♖xh7+ ♔g8 26 ♖xc7 fxg3 and Black's pieces become very active. Again the position is very hard to assess, but I think it is about equal; e.g., 27 hxg3 (if 27 fxg3 then 27...♘a6) 27...♗d4 and Black seems to be doing OK.

The text-move looks crazy (probably too crazy for most people), but I cannot see anything wrong with it.

19 ♖ad1!

This seems like White's best reply. Other moves:

a) 19 ♘c6 ♕c8 20 ♕xc8 ♖axc8 21 ♗e5 ♗xe5 22 ♘xe5 ♘xa1 23 ♖xa1 ♖cd8 is roughly equal. If anyone is better, then Black is, since his rooks will quickly attack the white pawns.

b) 19 ♗xg5 ♗xg5 20 ♕xa8 ♕xa8 21 ♗xa8 ♘xa1 (21...♗f6!? is also OK for Black, but not 21...♖xa8?? 22 ♘f7+) 22 ♗e4 (if 22 ♖xa1 then 22...♗f6!) 22...♘c2 23 ♗xc2 ♗xc2 24 f4 is again a very hard position to assess. Black's bishops and rook have a lot of potential but White's knight on e5 is a pain. Overall, I suspect it is roughly equal.

19...♘xe1! 20 ♖xd8 ♖axd8 21 ♕xc7 ♖d1! 22 ♗f1 ♗e4! 23 ♗xg5

If 23 ♗e3 then Black can continue 23...♘f3+ 24 ♘xf3 ♗xf3 followed by 25...♗e2.

23...♗xg5 24 f4 ♗f6 (D)

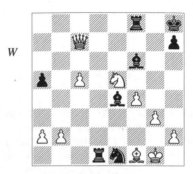

Assessing this position is very difficult. An extremely complicated battle lies ahead.

D2)

10 bxc3

This is White's simplest way to play. His c-pawns are more of a strength than a weakness, and he is trying to force e4.

10...♘c6! (D)

This position has only been reached once in practice, which shows how unique and unexplored the Classical Dutch is.

11 d5

This is the critical move, although it has not yet been tried in practice. Other moves allow Black to play 11...e5!.

The sole practical example featured 11 e4?!, when 11...e5 leaves Black at least equal. However, Black instead played 11...fxe4?, which is a basic mistake and gives White the edge.

11...♘e5 (D)

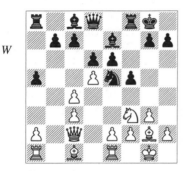

W

It looks at first like White should be able to keep an edge here, but it is not clear whether this is true.

12 ♘d4

Other moves are not convincing for White either. For example:

a) 12 dxe6 ♘xc4 13 e4 f4 (keeping the e-file closed) 14 ♗xf4 ♗xe6 15 ♘d4 (if White plays 15 e5 then 15...d5 16 ♘d4 ♕d7 17 ♖ad1 c6 is fine for Black) 15...♗f7 16 e5 dxe5 17 ♗xe5 ♘xe5 18 ♖xe5 ♗f6 =.

b) 12 ♘xe5 dxe5 13 ♖d1 ♗c5 =. Black will continue with ...♕e7, and if White captures on e6 then the simple ...c6 allows Black to recapture on e6 at some point. For example, 14 dxe6 ♕e7.

12...♘xc4 13 dxe6

If 13 ♘xe6 ♗xe6 14 dxe6, then 14...d5! gives White problems holding on to the e-pawn in the long run. 14...d5 is an important move since it prevents White from playing e4, supports the c4-knight, and blunts the power of the g2-bishop.

13...d5 14 ♘xf5 ♗xe6 15 ♘xe7+ ♕xe7 16 e4

Now 16...♕c5 is equal; Black's strong knight on c4 compensates for White's bishop-pair. 16...♗f7 also appears OK for Black.

2 The Ilyin-Zhenevsky System with 7...♕e8

1 d4 f5 2 c4 e6 3 ♘f3 ♘f6 4 g3 ♗e7 5 ♗g2 0-0 6 0-0 d6 7 ♘c3 ♕e8 *(D)*

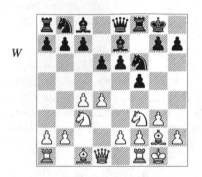

W

This is the most commonly played move. Black often transfers his queen to the kingside via h5 in search of attacking chances, while the other idea behind this move is to play ...♗d8 and ...e5. Black has to be careful when carrying out this manoeuvre if White plays b3 since he must then look out for ♗a3 ideas, with a potential attack against Black's f8-rook. After 7...♕e8 the d8-square is also available for Black's queen's knight in the event of the sequence ...♘c6, d5 ♘d8, which can be useful in some cases.

White now has many options:

A: 8 ♕c2?!   33
B: 8 ♖e1   35
C: 8 b3!   40

Or:

a) 8 ♘e1?! allows Black to play the desired 8...e5, equalizing. 9 dxe5 dxe5 10 ♘d5 ♗d8 11 b3 c6 12 ♘xf6+ ♗xf6 13 ♗a3 ♖f7 14 ♕c2 ♗e6 15 ♖d1 ♘d7 16 ♗d5!? cxd5 17 cxd5 ♗xd5 18 ♖xd5 ♘b6 19 ♖d1 ♖c8 20 ♕b1 and Black is very comfortable, Moskalenko-Glek, Lvov U-26 1985.

b) 8 b4?! e5 9 dxe5 dxe5 and then:

b1) 10 ♘d5 ♗d8 11 ♗b2 e4 with equality.

b2) 10 ♘xe5 ♗xb4 11 ♕b3 (Spraggett-Vallieres, Pere Noel 1983) and now Black should play 11...♘a6 =.

c) 8 ♗g5?! ♘e4 9 ♗xe7 and now in comparison to Line A of Chapter 1 (7...a5 8 ♗g5), Black does not have to recapture immediately on e7, but can instead play 9...♘xc3! 10 bxc3 ♕xe7 ∓, when White has no compensation for his doubled c-pawns, and Black will soon play ...e5. For example, 11 ♕d3 ♘c6 12 ♘d2 e5 13 e3 ♗d7 14 ♘b3 f4!? (an interesting attempt at creating play on the kingside) 15 exf4 exf4 16 c5 ♕f7 (planning to place the queen on its rightful square, h5) 17 ♗e4 ♕h5 18 cxd6 cxd6 19 ♘d2 ♖f6 20 ♗f3 ♗g4 21 ♗xg4 ♕xg4 22 ♕f3 ♕h3 23 ♘e4 ♖h6 24 ♕g2 ♕h5 25 g4 ♕h4 26 ♖ab1 ♖g6 27 h3 h5 28 f3 ♘a5

29 ♔h2 ♘c4 and Black has a decisive advantage, Rossolimo-Pachman, Hilversum 1947.

A)
8 ♕c2?!

White again wants to force through e4, but Black has an active reply that ensures him an easy game:

8...♕h5!

Now that the white queen has vacated the d1-h5 diagonal, Black can place his queen on h5 without worrying about it being exchanged after e3 and ♘e1.

Plans with ...♘c6 aren't effective any more since Black has no pawn on a5 to support the knight on b4. For example, after 8...♘c6? 9 d5! ♘b4 10 ♕b3 ± the black knight has to move so there is no time for Black to play ...e5.

Now (after 8...♕h5) White has two ways of playing:

A1: 9 e4   33
A2: 9 b3   34

Other moves do not promise White anything either:

a) 9 b4 ♘c6 10 b5 ♘d8 11 a4 ♘f7 12 ♗a3 g5 gives Black enough counterplay on the kingside, with ...g4 and ...♘g5 to follow. ...f4 is another possibility White has to worry about.

b) 9 ♗g5 leaves the bishop as a target on g5. Black can take advantage of this by 9...e5!?, which has not yet been played before, but it is natural and gives Black an equal game. Play might continue 10 dxe5 dxe5 11 ♗xf6 ♗xf6 12 ♘d5 ♕f7 =, when Black has no worries.

A1)
9 e4

This is White's most straightforward move. However, Black has two ways of reaching equality, one more ambitious than the other.

9...e5 (D)

This is the most ambitious move, but 9...fxe4 is the simplest route to equality: 10 ♘xe4 e5 11 dxe5 dxe5 12 ♘xf6+ ♗xf6 13 ♗e3 ♘c6 =.

10 dxe5 dxe5

Black can already claim to have achieved equality.

11 ♘d5

Other moves won't have Black quaking in his boots either:

a) 11 ♘xe5? fxe4 ∓ and White's e5-knight is looking lost.

b) 11 exf5 and then:

b1) 11...♗xf5?! 12 ♕b3 ♘bd7 is a risky option that involves a pawn sacrifice. There is no need for this, since Black's position was already perfectly OK. Then 13 ♗e3? e4 gave Black a good game in Rossiter-J.Rogers, British Ch (Eastbourne) 1991, but White should grab the b7-pawn with 13 ♕xb7; the saying 'If your position is bad anyway you might as well take as much material as you can', springs to mind. Black has some compensation after either 13...♗d6 or 13...♗d3 but it is doubtful whether he has enough play for the pawn.

b2) 11...♘c6 = is fine for Black.

c) 11 ♗g5 ♘c6 (11...fxe4 = is a sound alternative) 12 ♖fe1 f4!? 13 gxf4 and now either 13...♗h3 or 13...♗g4 gives Black plenty of compensation; for example, 13...♗g4 14 ♘d2 ♘d4 15 ♕a4 (if 15 ♕d3 then 15...♖ad8) 15...h6 and Black has enough play for the pawn.

11...♘xd5

White can now recapture in two different ways, but neither troubles Black at all.

12 cxd5

12 exd5 allows Black a nice edge:

a) 12...♗f6 is good: 13 c5 e4 14 ♘e1 ♘d7 ∓ Kozlovskaya-Kakabadze, USSR wom Ch (Sochi) 1971.

b) 12...♘d7 13 ♗d2 a5 14 ♖fe1 ♗f6 15 ♗c3 e4 ∓ 16 ♘d2 ♘e5 17 ♕d1 ♕f7 18 ♗f1 ♗d7 19 f3 ♕g6 20 f4 ♘g4 21 ♗g2?? ♗xc3 22 bxc3 ♕b6+ 0-1 Pelsser-Moser, Austrian Cht 2000.

12...♗d6 *(D)*

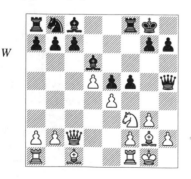

Black has an easy game here, and might even be a bit better.

13 exf5

Or 13 ♗e3 f4 (13...♘a6 = is also fine for Black) 14 ♗c5 ♘a6 15 b4 ♗g4 16 ♕c3 b6 17 ♗xd6 cxd6 18 a3 ♖ac8 ∓ Fromm-E.Moser, Bundesliga wom 2000/1. Black has a nice bind on the position.

13...♗xf5 14 ♕b3

And not 14 ♕c4? (Kelly-Kobalia, Menorca U-18 Wch 1996) 14...♗g4 15 ♘g5 ♗e2 ∓.

14...♘d7

Black is a little better. His pieces are ready for action, while the e-pawn is more of a strength than a weakness. Note that White must avoid playing 15 ♕xb7? in view of 15...♘c5 followed by 16...♗e4!.

A2)
9 b3

This may be White's best move, and was played by Botvinnik.

9...♘c6 10 ♗a3

White aims to prevent Black from ever advancing with ...e5 but on a3 the white bishop can become a target for tactics. For example, after the sequence e4 fxe4, ♕xe4 d5! White's a3-bishop is lost.

Other moves:

a) 10 d5?! ♘b4 11 ♕b1 e5 with an equal position.

b) 10 ♗b2 ♗d7 11 a3 and now:

b1) 11...♖ae8 (this is risky) 12 d5! ♘d8 13 ♘d4 e5!? 14 ♘db5 ♘f7 15 ♘xc7 ♖c8 16 ♘e6 ♗xe6 17 dxe6 ♘g5 (White's kingside looks exposed but he is material up) and now:

b11) 18 ♘d5 ♘xd5 19 ♗xd5 f4 20 f3? fxg3 21 hxg3 ♛h3 22 ♔f2? ♘xf3! and Black's attack proved too strong in Taimanov-Korchnoi, Leningrad 1950.

b12) 18 ♗xb7! is more challenging. After 18...♘g4 19 h4 ♘h3+ 20 ♔g2 the position looks very dangerous for White but it is difficult to find a good follow-up for Black.

b2) 11...♘d8 is Black's safest option. Play might continue 12 e4 fxe4 (12...♗c6 13 ♘d2 may leave White with a small advantage) 13 ♘xe4 e5 14 ♘xf6+ ♗xf6 15 dxe5 dxe5 with equality.

10...♘d8!

This has only been tried once, but looks like Black's best move. It also sets up some vicious traps for White. The idea is to play ...♘f7, where the knight is well placed, supporting an eventual ...e5 and can also prove useful jumping to g5 after the pawn push ...g5-g4. 10...♘e4?! is interesting but White gets an advantage after 11 ♘b5! ♗d8 12 d5!.

11 ♖fe1

Other moves:

a) 11 e4? falls for a nasty tactic: 11...fxe4 12 ♘xe4? ♘xe4 13 ♛xe4 d5! and Black wins White's a3-bishop.

b) 11 ♘b5?! ♗d7! and now the best move for White is probably 12 ♘c3, since 12 ♘xc7? loses a piece to 12...♖c8.

c) 11 e3 ♘f7 and Black should now continue with either ...c6, ...♖e8 and ...e5 or else ...g5, ...g4 and ...♘g5 – in both cases Black has active play.

11...♘f7 12 e4 fxe4 13 ♘xe4 *(D)*
13...e5!

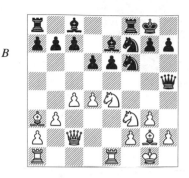

B

Black activates his light-squared bishop. Other moves are less convincing; e.g., 13...♘xe4 14 ♖xe4 d5 is a mistake due to 15 ♖h4! ♗xh4 16 ♗xf8 ♗f6 17 ♗a3 c6, when Black's backward e-pawn gives White the advantage.

14 ♘xe5

14 dxe5 is a mistake owing to the reply 14...♘xe4, when Black wins material after either 15 ♖xe4 ♗f5 or 15 ♛xe4? d5!.

14...♘xe5 15 dxe5 ♘g4 16 h3 ♘xe5

Black has a good deal of pressure against White's kingside.

B)
8 ♖e1

This is the most direct move. White aims to achieve the positionally favourable e4 advance, but with correct play Black's chances seem to be equal.

8...♛g6

Or:

a) The immediate 8...♘c6 may be a mistake since it gives White the option of playing 9 d5.

b) 8...♘e4?! is the normal reaction to ♖e1, but in this instance White may be able to get an advantage with normal moves: 9 ♘xe4 fxe4 10 ♘d2 d5 11 f3! (if, as is the case here, Black is forced to exchange on f3 in this type of position, then he can expect to be positionally worse) 11...exf3 (11...♗f6? fails to 12 fxe4 ♗xd4+ 13 e3 ±) 12 ♘xf3 ±.

9 e4 fxe4 10 ♘xe4 ♘xe4 11 ♖xe4 ♘c6 (D)

Black plans ...e5, which would give him an active position.

Instead, 11...♕xe4?! 12 ♘h4 is a bit embarrassing for her majesty, although Black does get a rook, knight and pawn for the queen. 12...♕xh4 13 gxh4 ♗xh4 14 ♗e3 ♘c6 and now:

a) 15 d5? (Black's pieces now come to life) 15...♘e5 16 dxe6 ♗xe6 17 f4 ♘xc4 18 ♗d5 ♗f7 19 ♗f2 ∓ San Segundo-Cenal Gutierrez, Spanish Ch (Barcelona) 2000.

b) White should play 15 ♗e4! ♗f6 16 ♕d3 h6 17 ♔h1 ±. It would take a brave or foolish man to try this line again as Black!

White now has a number of moves, but Line B3 is the only dangerous possibility:

B1: 12 ♖c3   37
B2: 12 ♖e1   38
B3: 12 ♕e2   39

Or:

a) 12 ♖e2?! is a strange square for the rook. Then:

a1) 12...e5?! is a somewhat unnecessary pawn sacrifice, since Black can get a nice game with normal play. 13 dxe5 ♗g4 14 exd6 ♗xd6 15 ♕d5+ ♔h8 and now White should play 16 ♘h4! ±. Instead, 16 h3? ♗xf3 17 ♗xf3 ♖xf3 18 ♕xf3 ♘d4 19 ♕e3 ♘xe2+ 20 ♕xe2 ♖e8 21 ♕f3 (21 ♗e3 may be better, since 21...♗xg3 is met by 22 ♕g4, when the subsequent exchange of queens favours White) 21...♖e1+ 22 ♔g2 ♕c2 (22...h6! is a better move, giving the black king an escape square) 23 ♕f7? (a blunder; 23 b3 {intending ♗b2} looks at least OK for White; for example, if Black plays 23...♖xc1?? then 24 ♕e3 +− exploits Black's back rank) 23...♕e4+ 24 ♕f3 ♖g1+ 0-1 was Drewalius-Seiler, Bonn 1998.

a2) 12...♗f6! followed by 13...e5 gives Black equality.

b) 12 ♘h4?! is premature, and the knight normally returns to f3 quickly. Black has an easy game after this. 12...♕f7 (there is no reason for Black to swap his bishop for the lousy knight on h4) and here:

b1) 13 ♗e3 ♗f6 = and Black will play 14...e5. White's knight and rook are looking rather stupid.

b2) 13 ♖f4 ♗f6 14 ♘f3 h6 (stopping any tricks with ♘g5) 15 ♖e4 (White has effectively lost a couple of tempi for no good reason) 15...e5! 16

d5 ♗f5 17 ♖e2 ♘b4 18 ♘e1 ♛g6 ∓
Savon-Katalymov, Novgorod 1961.

b3) 13 ♛e2 makes most sense, but
Black still has a comfortable position:

b31) 13...♗f6 14 ♘f3 h6 and now:

b311) 15 ♗d2 is similar to Line
B3, but Black's queen is better on f7
because it can't get hit by ♘h4. Black
should continue 15...e5 =, rather than
15...d5?! 16 ♖g4 e5? 17 ♘xe5! ±.

b312) 15 h4!? e5 16 dxe5 and now
16...♘xe5 = is very safe for Black. Instead, 16...dxe5?! is a mistake due to
17 g4! ± F.Portisch-Gyorgy, Harkany
2000.

b32) 13...e5 = is safe, and the most
natural reply.

B1)

12 ♖e3

This rook move need not worry
Black.

12...♗f6

White now has two sensible moves:

B11: 13 b3   37
B12: 13 d5   37

The latter is the more ambitious.

B11)

13 b3 e5

13...♘b4!? is an interesting idea:
Black wants to play ...e5 or even ...c5
next move depending on what White
plays. However, the text-move gives
Black comfortable equality.

14 ♗b2 e4! (D)
15 ♘d2

Other moves don't worry Black either; e.g., 15 ♘e1?! ♗f5 ∓ and Black
will follow up with ...♖ae8 and ...♗g5
if allowed.

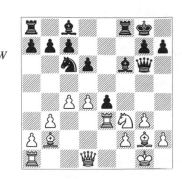

W

After the text-move (15 ♘d2) Black
has a few good replies:

a) 15...♘xd4 16 ♘xe4 ♘f3+ 17
♖xf3 ♗xb2 18 ♖xf8+ ♔xf8 =.

b) 15...♗xd4 is the safest way to
achieve a nice position. After 16 ♗xd4
♘xd4 17 ♘xe4 c5 ∓ Black's monster
of a knight on d4 ensures him a good
game. The game Fricker-Winiwarter,
Reggio Emilia 1958 continued 18 ♘c3
♗g4 19 ♗e4 ♛h5 20 ♛d3 ♖xf2 and
Black won on move 29.

c) 15...♗g4 16 ♗xe4 ♗xd1 17
♗xg6 hxg6 18 ♖xd1 ♗xd4 19 ♗xd4
♘xd4 and Black can continue with
...c5 and claim a small advantage.

B12)

13 d5

Now there are two ways for Black
to reply. The choice is a matter of personal preference.

13...exd5

13...♘d8 is the safer option: Black
wishes to play ...e5 with a pleasant position. 14 ♘d4 e5 15 ♘b5 ♛f7 16 ♖e1
♗f5 17 ♗e3 b6 18 b4 ♛d7 19 ♖c1
♘f7 20 ♘c3 ♘g5 21 f3 h5 = R.Wein-
stein-Sherwin, USA Ch (New York)
1958/9.

The text-move is more dangerous for both players, as White has a nice pawn-structure and pressure against Black's queenside, but Black has the more active pieces and open f- and e-files to work on.

14 cxd5 ♘e5 15 ♘xe5 ♗xe5 16 ♖b3 ♗f5!? 17 ♖xb7 ♗c2 18 ♕d2 ♖ae8 19 ♖xc7

19 f4 is probably better so White can place the queen on f2 in some lines.

19...♗d3 20 ♕b4 a5 21 ♕a4 ♗xg3! *(D)*

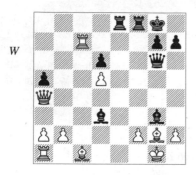

22 hxg3 ♖e1+ 23 ♔h2 ♗e4 24 ♗e3 ♕h5+ 25 ♗h3 ♖xe3 26 ♖xg7+ ♔xg7 27 ♕d4+ ♔g8 28 ♕xe3 ♗f5 29 g4 ♗xg4 30 ♖g1 ♖xf2+ 31 ♔h1 ♕xd5+ 32 ♗g2 ♕h5+ 33 ♗h3 ♕d5+

From here, the game Koblencs-Tal, Riga 1957 eventually ended in a draw – typical Tal adventures in the Classical Dutch!

B2)
12 ♖e1

The rook is less active on e1, and as we shall see, it is still not safe from Black's minor pieces.

12...♘b4!?

This aggressive thrust seems to be Black's best way of testing White's idea.

13 ♖e2

Other moves leave White with a bad position:

a) 13 ♗d2?! ♘c2 14 ♘h4 ♗xh4 15 ♗e4 ♘xe1! 16 ♗xg6 ♘f3+ 17 ♔g2 hxg6 18 gxh4 ♘xh4+ 19 ♔g1 ♘f3+ 20 ♔g2 ♘xd4 21 ♗a5 c5 22 ♗c7 ♘f5 ∓ Reilly-Heidenfeld, Ireland 1968 (22...b6!? also looks worrying for White).

b) 13 a3?! is again asking for it: 13...♘c2 14 ♘h4 ♗xh4 15 ♗e4 ♘xe1! 16 ♗xg6 ♘f3+ 17 ♔h1 hxg6 18 gxh4 b6 (there is some fun to be had on the a8-h1 diagonal!) 19 ♕e2 ♗b7 ∓ 20 ♕xe6+ ♔h7 21 d5 ♖ae8 22 ♕d7 ♖e1+ 23 ♔g2 ♖g1+ 0-1 E.Rayner-Quigley, London 1978.

13...♕h5! *(D)*

Black used to sacrifice a pawn with 13...e5 but this idea was never really justified. The text-move increases the pressure on the d1-h5 diagonal and prepares a later ...♗g4.

14 ♕b3 ♘c6 15 ♗d2 ♗f6

Again ...e5 is the all-important move for Black to play.

16 ♗c3 e5 17 c5+ ♔h8 18 d5?!

I never like this move, since Black need never worry about his centre now, and can concentrate on the kingside.

18...♘d8 19 cxd6 cxd6 20 ♖ee1 ♘f7 21 ♗d2 ♗g4 22 h4

Straat-Bellin, Wijk aan Zee 1975. Now Black should play 22...g5 =.

B3)

12 ♕e2

This is the only way for White to try for an advantage.

12...♗f6 *(D)*

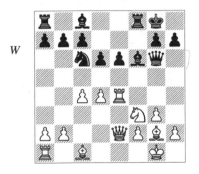

W

White has played two moves here:

B31: 13 ♗f4   39
B32: 13 ♗d2   39

B31)

13 ♗f4

This move, aimed against ...e5, has a drawback, but it is better than its reputation.

13...d5! 14 cxd5

Or 14 ♖xe6?! ♗xe6 15 ♕xe6+ ♔h8 16 ♘e5, and now 16...♗xe5?! 17 ♕xg6 hxg6 18 dxe5 dxc4 is merely OK for

Black, C.Petersen-Richters, Germany tt 1994. Black should play 16...♕e8! 17 ♕xd5 ♖d8 18 ♕c5 ♘xd4 ∓.

14...exd5 15 ♖e3

Black is fine in this position.

15...♗xd4

15...♗g4 = is also OK for Black, and may be more challenging than the text-move. For example, if White plays 16 ♕b5 then Black can respond with 16...♔h8.

16 ♘xd4 ♘xd4 17 ♕d2

17 ♗xd5+?! allows Black's pieces to become too active after 17...♔h8 with ideas of ...♗f5 and ...♖ad8 to follow.

Now (after 17 ♕d2):

a) 17...c5? was met by 18 ♖c1? in Iliushin-N.Pert, Oropesa del Mar U-18 Wch 1998, but White can gain a big advantage by 18 ♗xd5+ ♔h8 19 ♗e5! ± Budnikov-Fominykh, Voronezh 1988.

b) 17...♘e6 is almost equal; e.g., 18 ♕xd5 ♕f7.

B32)

13 ♗d2

This is White's most popular continuation, after which Black has to defend accurately.

13...e5

13...d5?! is a mistake. Black wants to invade White's position with his queen, but the problem is Black's lack of development and weakened kingside. 14 ♖f4 (14 cxd5? straightens out Black's pawn-structure and allows his dormant light-squared bishop to spring to life after 14...exd5) 14...♕c2 15 cxd5! (note that 15 b3? is a mistake due to 15...♕b2) 15...♕xb2? (this move loses,

but 15...exd5 allows 16 ♘g5! ±) 16
♖e1 exd5 17 ♘g5! and Black could not
successfully defend his king in Gla-
dyszev-Ellison, Isle of Man 2000.

14 dxe5 ♘xe5

14...dxe5?! is more dynamic and is
the move to play if Black needs to win
at all cost, but White should keep an
advantage with correct play: 15 ♗c3
♗f5 16 ♘h4 ♗xh4 17 ♖xh4 ± ♖ae8
18 ♕e3 h6 (Black's plan is to play
...g5 trapping the white rook on h4, but
White need not worry about this plan
if he plays correctly) 19 b4 (19 ♖e1?!
♘d4 makes things more complicated
than they need be) 19...♕f6 20 b5 ♘d8
21 c5! ± Yakovich-Diachkov, Russian
Clubs Cup (Maikop) 1998. White's
rook can swing over to a4.

**15 ♘xe5 ♗xe5 16 ♗c3 ♗xc3 17
bxc3**

White's activity and pressure on the
e-file offset his pawn-structure.

17...♗d7!? (D)

This seems to be better than the
more commonly played 17...c6, which
unnecessarily weakens the d6-pawn
and allows White to achieve a slight
advantage with 18 ♖e7. The text-move
keeps the pawn-structure intact.

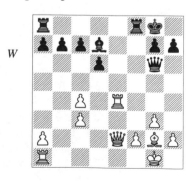

18 ♖e7

The only game I could find where
Black played 17...♗d7!? continued
18 ♖e1 but Black achieved complete
equality after 18...♖ae8 19 c5 ♗c6 20
♖xe8 ♖xe8 21 ♕c4+ ♔f8 22 ♖xe8+
♕xe8 = Liebert-I.Farago, Solo 1975.

18...♖ae8 19 ♗xb7 c6

This position is critical for the eval-
uation of 8 ♖e1. White has an extra
pawn but his bishop is shut out of the
game and his queenside pawns and
kingside are weak. Maybe White is
slightly better, but the game should
end in a draw. Play might continue:

a) 20 ♖e3 ♖xe3 21 ♕xe3 ♕c2 is
equal; ...♕b2 is a serious threat.

b) 20 c5 ♖xe7 (other options include 20...d5!? and 20...♗g4 21 ♕e3
♖xe7 22 ♕xe7 ♕f5 23 ♕e3 ♗f3 24
♖e1 dxc5) 21 ♕xe7 ♕f5 22 ♖f1 dxc5.

C)

8 b3! (D)

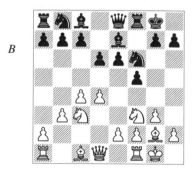

This prophylactic move is aimed at
preventing an eventual ...e5 by Black.
8 b3 is a slower but safer move than 8
♖e1. White's dark-squared bishop frequently moves to a3, where it aims at

stopping ...e5. 8 b3 seems to be the only way that White can achieve an advantage.

8...♘bd7

Black wants to play ...e5 at the right moment. This is also a useful waiting move, and is similar in spirit to the line we examined in Line C of Chapter 1. The plan is to meet White's pawn advance e4 with ...f4 so as to gain space on the kingside. This is one of Black's riskier plans, and this is also a rare move in tournament practice. White may be able to achieve a slightly better position with correct play.

One of the alternatives demands very serious consideration:

a) 8...♛h5? is just what White is looking for, since 9 ♗a3! ± puts a stop to ...e5 ideas.

b) 8...♗d8? is again a typical mistake, as White can get a bind by 9 ♗a3! ±.

c) 8...a5 is the most common move in this position, but White can get an advantage without too much risk after 9 ♗b2.

d) 8...♘e4!? is an interesting move, but I could only find eight examples of it in MegaBase 2001. The plan is similar to that in Line C of Chapter 1 but here Black has not played ...a5, which may be to his advantage. This is probably Black's safest option. Then White can try:

d1) 9 ♗b2 ♘xc3 10 ♗xc3 ♘d7 11 ♛d3 ♛h5 12 e4 f4! and Black is practically a tempo up on the variations given in Line C of Chapter 1, since ...♘d7 is more of a useful move than ...a5 in this type of position.

d2) After 9 ♛c2 ♘xc3 10 ♛xc3 the queen will have to move again since it will become exposed on the a1-h8 diagonal to Black's dark-squared bishop. 10...♗f6 11 ♗b2 ♘c6 (11...c5?! is generally a mistake in positions such as this since White can easily defend against the threats on the long diagonal, and ...c5 just weakens Black's central pawn-structure) 12 ♛d2 e5 =.

d3) 9 ♘xe4! is the critical response, but surprisingly it has not yet been played. After 9...fxe4 10 ♘e1 ♛g6!? (instead of playing ...d5 straight away, Black retains the option of ...e5) 11 ♛c2 d5 (on c2, the queen takes away the natural square for the white knight) 12 f3 (after 12 cxd5?! exd5 13 ♛xc7? ♘c6, ...♗d6 will seriously embarrass the white queen) 12...♘c6 13 e3 ♗f6 14 ♗b2 ♗g5 15 ♛e2 b6 16 ♘c2 exf3 17 ♗xf3 ♗a6 White may be slightly better since he has a nice centre, but Black exerts a good deal of pressure against White's centre. Practical examples are needed.

9 ♗b2 ♛h5

This is a good square for the queen, where it eyes White's king.

Again 9...♘e4 is a possible option; the exchange of knights would relieve Black's cramped position, but here White can successfully capture on e4, which leaves Black with some positional problems:

a) 10 ♛c2 ♘xc3 11 ♗xc3 ♛h5 12 e4 f4 is OK for Black.

b) 10 ♘e1?! (the only game featuring 9...♘e4 continued this way; White should keep his hold on e5 though) 10...♘df6 11 ♘b5 ♗d8 12 ♘d3 a6 13

♘a3 ♘g4 14 ♘c2 ♛h5 15 h3 ♘gf6 16 e3 ♛h6 and Black has sufficient play against White's weakened kingside, Nisman-Geliy, Planernaya 1981.

c) 10 ♘xe4! (the only serious threat to Black's play) 10...fxe4 11 ♘e1 is critical, and unplayed as yet. The difference between this line and 8...♘e4 is that Black no longer has the option of moving his knight to c6, but whether this makes a big difference is yet to be seen. After 11...d5 12 f3 White holds a small advantage. If Black captures on f3, White has more space and the stronger centre; White's plan will be to advance e4 at some point.

10 ♛c2

Now ...♘e4 is not an option for Black.

10 ♖e1 is less good, since Black can then play 10...♘e4. This is nearly always a good way of meeting ♖e1; exchanges also help Black because his position is more cramped than White's. 11 ♘xe4?! (as a rule, this capture is only worth playing when White can drop his knight back to e1; here we see a good example why) 11...fxe4 12 ♘d2 e3!? (an interesting idea – Black sacrifices a pawn for the initiative) 13 fxe3 ♗g5 14 ♘f1 ♘f6 15 h3 (the knight was going to g4) 15...e5 16 dxe5 dxe5 17 ♗xe5 ♗xh3 ∓ Borisenko-Lazarević, Leningrad 1964. Black is breaking through to the white king, while White's extra pawn does not look too healthy on e2.

After the text-move (10 ♛c2) Black has two options, which both have the same theme in mind: to counter e4 with ...f4.

C1: 10...♘g4   42
C2: 10...g5   43

The latter looks like the best test of White's play.

C1)

10...♘g4 (D)

In order to defend the f-pawn, so that e4 can be met by ...f4.

11 h3 ♘h6

White has two sensible plans here, both involving the e-pawn:

C11: 12 e4   42
C12: 12 e3   43

C11)

12 e4

This move is unplayed as yet.

12...f4

This is a hard position to assess. White has a large centre, but it is not clear what he can do with it. Black wants to play ...e5 at the right moment, but it is hard to play it straight away due to ♘d5, so he should play ...c6 first. Another plan is to play ...g5.

13 ♘e2!

This is probably the right plan since it makes Black decide what he is going to do with his f4-pawn. White is probably slightly better due to his space advantage.

Other moves shouldn't worry Black; for example:

a) 13 d5? only falls in with Black's plans: 13...e5.

b) If 13 ♕d2 then Black can reply 13...g5.

c) 13 g4 ♕g6 14 b4 ♘f7 and Black is OK.

C12)

12 e3

This is White's safest option, and the only two examples of 11...♘h6 in the database have continued this way. White's plan is to play ♘e2 with the idea of manoeuvring the knight to f4, which gives the kingside extra protection.

12...g5

12...♘f7 is a natural move but lets White play 13 e4! (other moves allow Black to play ...e5) at a time when Black can't reply ...f4. After 13...fxe4 14 ♘xe4 e5 White's better-placed pieces give him an edge.

13 ♘e2 c6 14 ♖fd1 ♘f6

Black should consider retreating his queen and trying to arrange ...g4 and ...e5, when things are far from clear.

15 ♘e1 ♗d7 16 ♘d3 ♘f7 17 ♕d2 ♖ae8

E.Grünfeld-Bogoljubow, Zandvoort 1936. White has more space and prospects of breaking with c5 or b4-b5, which gives him a small advantage.

C22)

10...g5!?

This has only been played once, but it looks like Black's best idea. The point is always to meet e4 with ...f4, when ...g4 and ...f3 is threatened, locking in the g2-bishop. The b2-bishop will also find it hard to activate itself on the a1-h8 diagonal. If White does nothing, Black will continue with ...g4 and ...e5.

11 e4

Other moves give Black no problems:

a) 11 d5?! might appear to be a good move since it looks as if 11...e5! is impossible due to 12 ♕xf5 (otherwise Black will have plenty of play with his kingside pawn-majority and active pieces), but Black has 12...♘g4, when White must try to escape with minimum damage:

a1) If 13 ♕e6+? White's queen will quickly run out of squares: 13...♖f7 14 h3 ♘df6 15 hxg4 ♘xg4 ∓.

a2) 13 ♕b1 ♖xf3 14 h3 ♖xf2 ∓ 15 ♖xf2 ♘xf2 16 ♔xf2 ♘f6 and White has to be careful. 17 g4? is a big mistake due to 17...♕h4+ 18 ♔g1 ♗xg4 ∓, while 17 ♕d3 is met by 17...♗xh3 18 ♖h1 g4. That leaves 17 ♕h1, when Black can be very satisfied with his position.

b) After 11 ♖fe1 g4! 12 ♘d2 (12 ♘h4 is poor since the knight becomes a target after 12...♘e8 ∓) 12...e5 = Black has enough play in the centre and on the kingside.

11...f4!? *(D)*

This unclear position awaits practical testing. I believe that the chances are about equal.

12 e5!

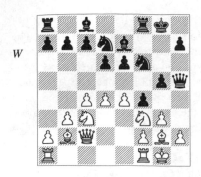

This is probably the critical test of the whole line. Other moves:

a) 12 h3 g4 13 hxg4 ♘xg4 exposes White to a great deal of danger.

b) 12 gxf4 gxf4 13 ♔h1 e5 14 ♘d5 ♗d8 15 ♖g1 ♘g4 16 h3 ♘df6 looks fine for Black.

12...dxe5 13 dxe5 ♘g4!?

This is Black's most active move, but it allows White to obtain a good square for his knight.

The alternative is 13...♘e8, which stops ♘e4 due to ...g4 and ...f3, but Black's pieces are passive and White can take advantage of this:

a) 14 gxf4 ♖xf4 15 ♘e1 ♖h4 gives Black sufficient play against White's kingside.

b) 14 ♘e2 g4 15 ♘xf4 ♖xf4 16 gxf4 gxf3 17 ♕d1! and White will gain a rook and two pawns for his two minor pieces, but Black is fine in all the ensuing positions due to White's weak f-pawns.

c) 14 h3! seems to be White's most dangerous move: he sacrifices a pawn to open up lines against Black's king.

After 14...fxg3 15 fxg3 g4 16 ♘h4! the position is quite complex, but I prefer White's chances due to the open nature of Black's king and the passive placing of his pieces.

14 ♘e4!

A very nice central square.

14...♘h6

With the idea of playing a quick ...g4.

15 gxf4 *(D)*

15 h3 g4 gives Black enough play on the kingside.

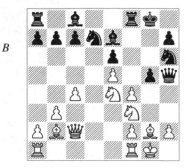

Now both captures on f4 deserve attention:

a) 15...gxf4 16 ♖ad1 is still very unclear but White's knight on e4 should give him the advantage.

b) 15...♖xf4 (this gives White the g3-square) 16 ♘g3 ♕f7 17 ♘e1 and White is slightly better due to Black's undeveloped queenside pieces, but an interesting battle lies ahead since Black can create pressure by bringing both his knights around to White's kingside.

3 The Ilyin-Zhenevsky System with 7...♞e4!

1 d4 f5 2 c4 e6 3 ♘f3 ♘f6 4 g3 ♗e7 5 ♗g2 0-0 6 0-0 d6 7 ♘c3 ♘e4! *(D)*

W

Since Black normally plays ...♘e4 anyway, it makes sense to move the knight to that square straight away. Surprisingly, 7...♘e4! is rare in practice, but it seems to solve all of Black's problems. The a5-square is reserved for possible use by the queen's knight (the sequence ...♘c6, d5 ♘a5 is common), while the black queen remains on d8 for now, where it can sometimes exert useful pressure against White's d4-pawn after a ...d5 advance. Another advantage of this move is that it makes it very hard for White to play e4. 7...♘e4 is the simplest way for Black to play, and the easiest to learn.

White now has a number of options:

A: 8 ♖e1!?   46
B: 8 ♘xe4   46
C: 8 ♕c2   46

Line C is the critical test.

Otherwise:

a) The passive 8 ♗d2 is not a move Black need fear; e.g., 8...♗f6 9 ♕c2 ♘xd2 = and ...e5 is Black's next move, when he has nothing to worry about.

b) 8 ♕d3 defends the c4-pawn, which would be useful if the black knight had to go to a5, but now it can move to e5 with tempo: 8...♘xc3 9 bxc3 ♘c6 10 d5 (or else Black plays ...e5 with the advantage) 10...♘e5 11 ♘xe5 (11 ♕d4 ♘xf3+ 12 ♗xf3 e5 ∓) 11...dxe5 12 dxe6 c6 =.

c) 8 ♕b3 is not as worrying for Black as Line C because Black is not forced to move his knight from e4. Then:

c1) 8...♘xc3 and now 9 bxc3 ♘c6 10 d5 ♘a5 11 ♕a4 transposes to Line C1 and 9 ♕xc3 to Line C2.

c2) 8...♗f6 9 ♘xe4 fxe4 10 ♘d2 ♗xd4 (10...d5? is a mistake due to 11 cxd5 exd5 12 ♘xe4) 11 ♗xe4 (Black now has a central pawn majority, but White's pieces are active and he is now threatening ♗xb7 and ♕d3) 11...♗b6 12 ♕c2 h6 13 e3 (Erwich-S.Williams,

Millfield 2002) 13...♘c6 with an equal position.

A)

8 ♖e1!?

This move has not yet been tried in practice. White is trying to play e4.

8...♘c6!?

This is an interesting idea, leading to positions similar to Line C1.

Black has other options depending on the type of position that he wants to aim for:

a) 8...♗f6 9 ♕c2 d5 is similar to a Stonewall, and is justified here.

b) 8...b6 is another sensible idea, when the bishop on b7 will give extra support to e4. This reaches positions with a Nimzo-Indian character.

9 d5

As usual, this is the only critical test when Black plays ...♘c6.

9...♘xc3 10 bxc3 ♘a5 11 ♕a4

Black's chances shouldn't be any worse.

B)

8 ♘xe4

This move releases the tension a bit prematurely.

8...fxe4 9 ♘e1

The other knight retreat, 9 ♘d2, makes little sense since it blocks the queen's defence of the d-pawn, and in any case the knight has little scope on d2. For example, 9...d5 10 f3, and then:

a) 10...exf3 11 ♘xf3 ♘c6 12 ♗e3 ♗f6 = Bromberger-Dobos, Bechhofen 1998.

b) 10...e3!? is another interesting option. Play might continue 11 ♘b1

dxc4 12 ♗xe3 ♗f6 =; the pressure on d4 and on the a1-h8 diagonal gives Black an easy game.

9...d5 10 f3 dxc4

The queen makes its presence felt.

11 fxe4 e5! *(D)*

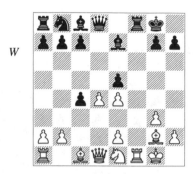

At this point Gebhard-K.D.Schulz, Germany 1998/9 continued 12 d5?! ♗c5+ 13 ♔h1 ♖xf1+ 14 ♗xf1 ♗g4 15 ♘c2 ♕f6 16 ♗e3 ♘d7 17 ♗g2 ∓. It is probably better to keep the tension with 12 e3 or 12 ♖xf8+ ♗xf8 13 e3 c5 =.

C)

8 ♕c2 ♘xc3

White now has two ways of recapturing:

C1: 9 bxc3   46
C2: 9 ♕xc3   48

C1)

9 bxc3 *(D)*

9...♘c6 10 d5

This is the only way to test Black's play. Other moves:

a) 10 ♖d1 (the black queen usually wants to move to h5 anyway, so this move does not help White) 10...♕e8

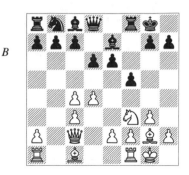

B

11 d5 ♘d8 12 e4 e5 is slightly better for Black.

b) 10 e4?! is a mistake owing to 10...e5 ∓, when Black is already a bit better due to White's doubled c-pawns. Black can also create an attack against the white king with ...f4. Play might continue 11 d5 ♘b8 (11...♘a5 is also OK for Black) 12 c5 (otherwise Black will play ...b6, ensuring that White's c-pawns are a weakness for the rest of the game) and now both 12...fxe4 and 12...♘a6 are good for Black.

10...♘a5!

Making use of White's doubled c-pawns.

11 ♕a4

Other moves need not worry Black:

a) After 11 ♘d2 e5 ∓ White's c-pawns are going to become a target.

b) 11 ♘d4 e5 12 ♘e6 ♗xe6 13 dxe6 and now Black has many ways to keep a slight edge. Probably the best is 13...c6, when White's c- and e-pawns are looking shaky: 14 e4 (if 14 ♕a4 then 14...♖f6) 14...f4 ∓.

c) 11 dxe6 is the most popular response. Then 11...♘xc4! (up to now, 11...♗xe6 has always been the move played in practice) 12 ♘d4 d5 gives

Black safe equality. Play might continue 13 ♘xf5 ♗xe6 14 ♘xe7+ ♕xe7 15 e4 ♕c5.

11...b6 12 dxe6

White's other option, 12 ♘d4 e5 13 ♘c6, does not promise him anything either. Black should reply 13...♗d7! 14 ♘xd8 ♗xa4 15 ♘e6 ♖fc8, when White is unable to defend his weak c-pawns.

12...♗xe6 13 ♘d4 ♗xc4 *(D)*

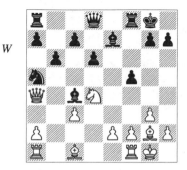

W

14 ♘c6

This is better than capturing the exchange straight away. After 14 ♗xa8 ♕xa8 ∓ Black has an advantage due to his better control of the position. Black can kick White's pieces back with his queenside pawns and exert pressure against the c3-pawn, while White's weakened kingside may also play a role. A possible continuation is 15 ♕c2 ♕e4! (Black need not fear the trade of queens since White's pawns will become weaker without his pieces gaining any more freedom) 16 ♕xe4 fxe4 17 ♖e1 ♗f6 with ...c5 and possibly ...d5-d4 to follow.

14...♕d7 15 ♘xe7+ ♕xe7 16 ♗xa8 ♖xa8 *(D)*

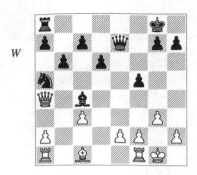

I think this position should be equal. Black has a pawn and a knight for the rook, which is enough in this case. The opposite-coloured bishops enhance Black's attacking chances. It is also hard to find a good square for White's bishop. Play might continue 17 ♖e1 ♕f6 18 ♕c2 ♗d5 19 ♗e3 c5 20 ♖ad1 ♗e4 21 ♕c1 (if the queen moves anywhere else it will be hit with ...♘c4 or the c3-pawn will drop) 21...h6 22 h4 (otherwise Black plays ...g5) 22...♘c4, when White's pieces are looking rather pathetic.

C2)
9 ♕xc3 (D)

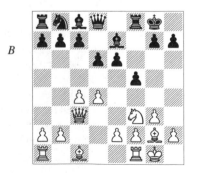

9...a5

This useful waiting move is aimed against White's plan of ♖e1 and e4. Now if the rook moves to e1, Black will have possibilities of playing ...e5, when after an exchange of pawns on e5, he threatens ...♗b4 winning the exchange. The pawn on a5 also prevents White from expanding with b4.

9...♗f6 is a reliable alternative. This natural and useful move puts the bishop on the same diagonal as the white queen. Black will force ...e5 while White does not have time to play e4. Then:

a) 10 b3?! makes little sense given that this pawn can move directly to b4, gaining more space. Black has a very easy game after 10...♘c6 11 ♗b2 e5 =; as usual, the push ...e5 guarantees Black equality, if not more.

b) 10 b4! (not just gaining space, but also deterring ...♘c6 because of b5) 10...♘d7 (the plan is to play ...e5, leading to positions where White's edge on the queenside is counterbalanced by Black's play in the centre and potentially on the kingside) and now, for example, 11 ♗b2 e5 12 dxe5 dxe5 13 c5 e4 14 ♘d4 ♘e5 gives Black a solid enough position. He can be happy with the outcome of the opening, but again practical examples are needed.

Now (after 9...a5) White has two independent continuations:
C21: 10 ♕c2   49
C22: 10 a3   49

10 ♖e1 transposes to Line D1 of Chapter 1, which is OK for Black, and which we studied in depth.

C21)
10 ♕c2

White wastes time to remove his queen from the e1-a5 diagonal. It is also useful on c2 to support the e2-e4 break. On the other hand, it leaves the d4-pawn less well defended and can become a target for Black's queen's knight, since a later ...♘d4 or ...♘b4 would gain a tempo.

10...♗f6! *(D)*

Unfortunately, the normal plan of 10...♘c6?! does not work here because of 11 d5!, which is always the move to keep a lookout for when the knight moves to c6. After 11...♘b4 12 ♕d2, if Black plays 12...e5 he loses the a-pawn for very little compensation: 13 a3 ♘a6 14 ♕xa5 ±.

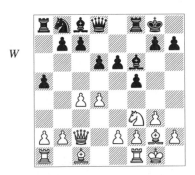

W

11 a3!?

Trying to stop Black's plan of playing ...♘c6 and ...♘b4, since White is now fully ready to meet ...♘c6 with d5.

The alternatives do little harm to Black:

a) 11 b3 ♘c6 12 ♗b2 e5 =.

b) 11 e4 ♘c6 (this ensures Black equality) 12 exf5 (the aggressive 12 d5

doesn't work here due to 12...♘b4 13 ♕e2 fxe4 14 ♕xe4 exd5 15 cxd5 ♖e8 ∓) 12...♘xd4 13 ♘xd4 ♗xd4 14 fxe6 ♗xe6 and here Black's bishops are strongly placed in the centre of the board, and I consider the game to be equal. Play might continue 15 ♗e3 (not 15 ♗xb7?!, when Black gets a very pleasant position after 15...♖b8 16 ♗d5 {if 16 ♗g2 then 16...♕f6} 16...♗xd5 17 cxd5 ♕f6) 15...♗xe3 16 fxe3 ♕g5 17 ♕d3 c6, when Black has ...♕e5 and ...♕c5 in reserve to hit White's e- and c-pawns, but he also has a weak d-pawn, so a fair result would be a draw.

11...e5

When the chance to play ...e5 is there, it is normally foolish not to take it.

12 dxe5 dxe5 13 e4

13 ♖d1 doesn't really help White since Black's queen was already heading towards h5: 13...♕e8 14 b3 e4 gives Black a slight advantage.

13...♕e8 14 exf5 ♕h5

Black's well-placed pieces make up for his isolated pawn on e5. I believe the position is equal. Note that 15 ♘d2?! (winning a pawn but at a price) 15...♘c6 16 ♗xc6 bxc6 17 ♕e4 ♗xf5 18 ♕xc6 ♕e2 is a little better for Black since White will miss the presence of his missing light-squared bishop; e.g., 19 ♕f3 ♕xf3 20 ♘xf3 ♗d3.

C22)
10 a3!

This is the only way to achieve anything from the opening.

10...♘c6

10...a4?! is a mistake since White can then force the thematic e4 with 11 ♖e1.

11 d5 ♗f6 12 ♕c2 ♘e7 13 dxe6 ♗xe6

Black's good bishops compensate for his slightly inferior pawn-formation. White may be slightly better due to his extra space, but it is nothing serious.

14 ♘g5! *(D)*

This is the only way to cause Black any problems.

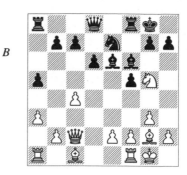

B

14...♗c8 15 ♖d1 a4

Black is only slightly worse.

4 Ilyin-Zhenevsky System: Deviations for White

In this chapter, we round up some early deviations for White. None of these are particularly scary for Black, if he follows basic principles and aims to play ...e5. White's ideas fall into four basic types:

1: White avoids playing c4
2: White plays an early ♘h3
3: White tries to play an early e4
4: White delays or avoids ♘c3

1 d4 f5 2 g3 ♘f6 3 ♗g2 e6

Now:

A: 4 ♘d2   51
B: 4 ♘f3   52
C: 4 c4   53

The first is one of the ways in which White can try to force through e4. In Line B we consider lines where White avoids c4. Line C covers a variety of ideas for White that have not been discussed in earlier chapters.

4 ♘c3?! is rather a lame move. White has the e4 push in mind, but if he wants to play this way then it is better to put the knight on d2. One reason for this is that Black can now play 4...d5, reaching a Stonewall structure where White can't play c4 due to his misplaced knight on c3 (this should be compared with Line C2 of Chapter 9,

to which 5 ♘f3 transposes). Black's other option is 4...♗b4. In both cases Black should have no problems.

A)

4 ♘d2 (D)

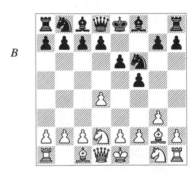

The idea behind this crafty move is to play a quick e4. Black must now be alert since normal developing moves allow White to obtain an advantage. For example, 4...♗e7 allows 5 e4!, when White is better. The disadvantage of having the knight on d2 is that d4 is undefended, and Black can try to make use of this:

4...c5!?

4...♘c6 5 c3 d5 is a more solid option for Black. The Stonewall set-up is fully OK here since White will have to waste a tempo playing c3-c4 at some

point. 6 ♘df3 ♗d6 7 ♗f4 0-0 8 ♘e5
♗d7 9 ♘gf3 ♗e8 10 0-0 ♘e4 11 ♘d3
g5 12 ♗e5 ♗g6 13 ♕c1 ♕e7 14 ♘fe1
h6 15 f3 ♘f6 16 ♗xf6 ♕xf6 17 f4 g4
is equal, Averbakh-Kholmov, Moscow
1969.

Now (after 4...c5):
a) 5 dxc5 ♗xc5 6 ♘b3 ♗b6 7 c4
♘c6 8 ♘f3 e5 9 0-0 d6 10 ♗g5 h6 11
♗xf6 ♕xf6 12 e3 0-0 13 ♖c1 ♖d8 14
♕e2 ♗e6 15 ♖fd1 ♗f7 16 ♘fd2 e4 17
♘b1 ♘e5 with a slight advantage for
Black, Summermatter-King, San Ber-
nardino 1991.
b) 5 c3 cxd4 6 cxd4 ♘c6 7 ♘gf3
♕b6 8 e3 ♕a6 9 ♗f1 ♕a5 = V.Kova-
čević-Sale, Solin 1996.

B)
4 ♘f3 ♗e7 5 0-0 0-0 *(D)*

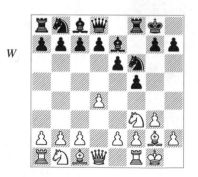

We consider two moves here:
B1: 6 b3   52
B2: 6 ♘bd2   53
In both these lines White wishes to
delay c4, sometimes in the hope of
playing ♖e1 and e4. The disadvantage
of this is that Black can put his queen's
knight on c6 without worrying about
the pawn advance d5.

B1)
6 b3
This move has some independent
value since White does not have to
play c4, and Black has other options
available to him. Play will normally
transpose to the standard lines with c4
though. Black can choose from a number of different plans here depending
on personal preference:
6...♘c6!?
Now that Black need not fear d5,
...♘c6 is a new option available to
him. Other moves:
a) 6...♘e4 (this is probably Black's
most reliable move, since the option of
playing ...d6 or ...d5 is left open) 7
♗b2 ♗f6 8 ♘bd2 c5 (8...♘c6 is a
solid alternative) 9 c4 ♘c6 10 ♕c2
♘b4 11 ♕c1 cxd4 12 ♘xe4 fxe4 13
♘xd4 d5 14 cxd5 exd5 15 a3 ♘a6 16
b4 ♕b6 17 ♕d2 ♘c7 ½-½ Bäckwin-
kel-Haub, 2nd Bundesliga 2001/2.
b) 6...a5 7 ♘bd2 (after 7 a3, 7...b6!?
8 ♘e5 ♖a7 with ...♗b7 to follow is an
interesting untried plan) 7...♘c6 8 ♗b2
a4 9 bxa4 ♖xa4 10 c4 ♖a6 11 d5 ♘a5
12 ♘d4 c5 13 ♘b5 d6 14 ♕c2 e5! = 15
a4 ♘e8 16 ♖a3 f4 17 ♘e4 ♗g4 18
♔h1 ♕d7 19 gxf4 exf4 20 ♖g1 ♕f5
gave Black good attacking chances
in Muse-Zaja, Croatian Cht (Tucepi)
1996.
7 ♗b2 d6 8 c4 ♘e4 9 ♕c2
9 d5 may be White's best option in
this line. Play becomes very interesting after 9...♗f6! 10 ♕c1, when Black
has a slightly compromised pawn-
structure but his pieces have found active squares.
9...♗f6 10 ♖d1 ♕e7 11 a3

Halkias-Viahas, Khania 1995. Black should now continue 11...e5 =, which looks natural and good.

B2)
6 ♘bd2 d6 *(D)*

The other option is the immediate 6...♘c6, which is OK, but it is then harder for Black to achieve the liberating move ...e5.

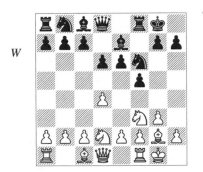

W

7 ♖e1

This need not worry Black as he can easily meet e4 with either ...f4 or ...e5 at the right moment.

Another option is 7 b3, and this move makes more sense than 7 ♖e1 since White wants to get a firm grip on the e5-square before taking any action himself. However, Black can reply 7...e5! (this is why Black plays 6...d6 instead of 6...♘c6: it gives him the option of playing ...e5 immediately) 8 dxe5 dxe5 9 ♘c4 (9 ♘xe5?? ♕d4 is the point of 7...e5!) 9...e4 = Gerusel-Clemens, W.German Ch (Bad Pyrmont) 1976. Now ...♗e6 and ...♘c6 will complete Black's development and give him a good game.

7...♘c6 8 e4 fxe4

This is the safest method of reaching equality. There is another interesting option: 8...f4!? (a novel pawn push which complicates matters) 9 e5 (otherwise Black will play ...e5) 9...dxe5 10 dxe5 ♘g4! 11 gxf4 ♘b4!? intending ...♘d5 and ...♘xf4, with interesting and roughly equal play.

9 ♘xe4 ♘xe4 10 ♖xe4 e5!

The game is equal. Black's pieces will become very active after a subsequent ...♗f5.

C)
4 c4 ♗e7
Now:

C1)
5 ♘h3?! *(D)*

B

This move is aimed against a Stonewall set-up, but with Black's pawn still on d7 Black can play ...d6, when an early ...e5 will leave White's knight looking misplaced. The only way the white knight can join in the game is by moving to f4 and then to d3 or d5 but

White loses a lot of time with this manoeuvre and in the meantime Black will obtain enough play in the centre.

5...0-0 6 0-0 d6! 7 ♘c3

Black now has two equally viable ways to play, and the choice between them is a matter of temperament.

C11: 7...e5   54
C12: 7...c6   54

C11)

7...e5 (D)

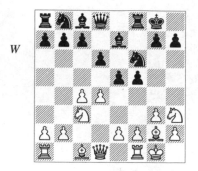

This is the simplest route to equality.

8 dxe5

8 c5?! is a crude attempt. This is normally only a good idea when Black has moved his c-pawn to c6; here he can always recapture on d6 with his c-pawn. 8...♘c6 9 cxd6 cxd6 10 dxe5 dxe5 11 ♕b3+ ♔h8 12 ♘g5 ♘d4 ∓ Frosch-E.Moser, Austrian Cht 2000/1. 13 ♘f7+? is not good due to 13...♖xf7 14 ♕xf7 ♗e6 winning White's queen.

8...dxe5 9 ♕xd8 ♗xd8!

This is more accurate than 9...♖xd8, since now the bishop can't get hit by ♘d5. The bishop will also find a nice diagonal on c7 or b6 after ...c6.

10 b3 c6 (D)

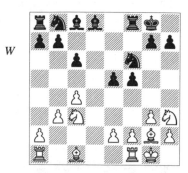

The position is equal. Black intends to develop normally with ...♗c7 or ...♗b6, ...♗e6, ...♘a6 or ...♘bd7 and ...h6 (...h6 denies White's knight the g5-square).

11 ♗a3

11 e4 ♗b6! (Black wants to place his bishop on d4 and deter White from playing f4; if White cannot play f4 then his h3-knight will have little chance to rejoin the battle) 12 ♘g5 h6 13 ♘f3 fxe4 14 ♘h4 ♗d4 ∓ Pereyra-Mellano, Mar del Plata 1993. Black is firmly in charge.

11...♖e8 12 ♖fd1 ♘a6 13 ♗d6 ♗c7 14 ♗xc7 ♘xc7 15 ♖d6 ♔f8 16 ♖ad1 ♔e7 17 e4 fxe4 18 ♘g5 ♗g4 19 ♖1d2 e3!

This is an important motif in this type of position: Black returns the extra pawn but his remaining e-pawn is now far less exposed.

20 fxe3 ♘e6

= Hoang Thanh Trang-E.Moser, Istanbul wom OL 2000.

C12)

7...c6 (D)

This leads to more complex positions than 7...e5.

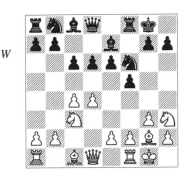

W

White now has three options:
C121: 8 ♕b3   55
C122: 8 e4   55
C123: 8 d5   56

C121)
8 ♕b3
This was Karpov's choice.
8...♘a6 9 ♘g5 e5 10 ♖d1
Other moves:

a) 10 c5+?! d5 ∓.

b) 10 dxe5!? can lead to an interesting and unclear position after the continuation 10...♘c5 11 exf6 ♘xb3 12 fxe7 ♕xe7 13 axb3.

10...♕e8 11 d5 h6 12 ♘f3
Black is doing fine, and can continue with a number of decent plans:

a) 12...c5 closes up the position and plans a kingside attack starting with ...♕h5.

b) 12...♘c5 (the most adventurous move) 13 ♕c2 ♘ce4 =.

c) 12...cxd5 13 ♘xd5 ♘xd5 14 ♖xd5 ♗e6 15 ♖d1 ♘c5 gives Black an active position, Karpov-P.Nikolić, Reykjavik 1991.

In all these cases Black's chances seem no worse, and it is a question of style which plan Black wants to follow.

C122)
8 e4 e5
This is natural, but 8...fxe4 also appears fine: 9 ♘xe4 e5 10 dxe5 dxe5 11 ♘hg5 ♕xd1 12 ♖xd1 ♗g4 13 ♖e1 =.
9 dxe5 dxe5 10 ♕e2
It is not in White's interest to exchange queens, since Black's minor pieces are more active than White's. Other moves:

a) 10 ♘g5 ♕xd1 (it's also possible for Black to play 10...h6 =) 11 ♖xd1 ♗c5 12 exf5 ♗xf5 = (Black's piece-play makes up for his isolated pawn) 13 ♗e3 ♗xe3 14 fxe3 ♘a6 15 h3 ♘b4 with an easy game for Black, Eslon-Ulybin, Zaragoza 1993.

b) 10 ♕xd8 ♖xd8 (10...♗xd8 is untried; Black will place his bishop on c7 or b6, and develop normally; play might continue 11 ♖e1 ♗c7 =) and then:

b1) 11 a3? is a mistake since after 11...h6 White's knight cannot return to the game via g5, leaving White in a difficult situation.

b2) 11 ♗g5 and now 11...♗e6?!, as played in Szabados-Rossolimo, Amsterdam 1950, allows 12 f4!. Black should prefer the simple 11...h6 12 ♗xf6 ♗xf6 13 ♖ad1 ♖xd1 (13...♖d4?! allows 14 f4!) 14 ♖xd1 ♘a6, when Black is at least equal; his bishop-pair may even give him a slight edge.

10...♕c7
I believe Black has equalized.

11 ♖e1

11 exf5 ♗xf5 12 ♘g5 ♘bd7 13 ♘ge4 ♘c5 14 ♘xc5?! (14 ♘xf6+ ♗xf6 15 ♘e4 ♘e6 16 b3 ♘d4 17 ♕b2 ♕f7 18 ♗e3 ♖ad8 is level, F.Portisch-Schmittdiel, Wattens 1999) 14...♗xc5 15 ♗e3 ♗d4! ∓ Merino Garcia-Arizmendi, Spanish Ch (Torrevieja) 1997.

11...♗b4 12 exf5 ♗xf5 13 ♗d2

Not 13 ♕xe5? ♕d7.

13...♕d7!

This move is an improvement over 13...♘bd7, which allowed 14 ♘d5! in R.Bagirov-Goloshchapov, St Petersburg 2000.

14 ♘g5 ♗d3 15 ♕xe5 ♘g4 16 ♕e6+ ♕xe6

Now:

a) If 17 ♖xe6 then 17...♘xf2 is good for Black.

b) 17 ♘xe6 ♖xf2 and Black can be happy with his position.

C123)

8 d5 e5 *(D)*

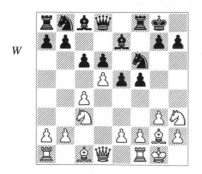

W

9 b4

9 e4 ♘a6 10 ♘g5 is weaker, and costs White a pawn: 10...h6 11 ♘e6 ♗xe6 12 dxe6 fxe4 13 ♘xe4 ♘c7 and

Black took the pawn and won on move 20 in Abbasov-Ulybin, Barlinek 2001. White's play is probably explained by concerns about what future the h3-knight had.

9...h6

9...♘e4!? is interesting, but less safe.

The text-move is not strictly needed but it is always nice to stop the h3-knight from entering the game.

10 dxc6 ♘xc6!?

This is the more active recapture. 10...bxc6 is probably also OK; play might then continue 11 b5 ♗b7 12 ♖b1 ♕d7 13 bxc6 ♗xc6 14 ♘d5 ♘xd5 15 ♗xd5+ ♔h8 =.

After the text-move (10...♘xc6) it is difficult to find anything that gives White any edge, and this is all due to the wayward knight on h3:

a) 11 ♘d5 ♘xd5 12 ♕xd5+ ♔h8 13 b5 ♘d4 14 e3 ♘e2+ 15 ♔h1 ♘c3 16 ♕d3 ♘e4 17 ♗a3 ♗e6 ∓ Palliser-S.Williams, Hampstead 1998. White is going to have a tough time defending his c-pawn.

b) 11 b5 is well met by 11...♘a5! (not 11...♘d4?, when 12 ♘f4! is troublesome for Black).

c) 11 a3 tries to keep the tension. Black should just develop normally; for example, 11...♗e6 12 ♘d5 ♕d7 13 f4 (Black was threatening ...f4 winning the h3-knight) 13...e4 =. White is playing without his h3-knight and g2-bishop. Black should aim to exchange on d5 at some point so that White has to recapture with his pawn, closing the half-opened d-file. Black would then have a nice position.

C2)

5 ♘c3

Here we focus on a rare line where White tries to disrupt Black's Ilyin-Zhenevsky set-up with a quick e4.

5...0-0!

Now Black will be able to play ...d7-d5 in one move in the event of White playing e4. This is better than 5...d6?!, since White then has 6 e4! ±.

6 e4?!

Of course, 6 ♘f3 d6 7 0-0 is the main line, and is covered in Chapters 1-3.

6...fxe4 7 ♘xe4 d5! *(D)*

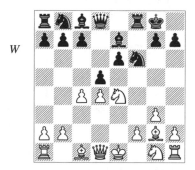

Making use of the move-order.

8 ♘xf6+ ♗xf6

Black has an easy game:

a) 9 ♘f3?! (Arkell-S.Williams, Oxford 1998) and now Black can get a pleasant advantage with the simple 9...dxc4 10 0-0 ♘c6, when Black is a sound pawn up with ideas like ...♘b4 and ...e5 floating around.

b) 9 cxd5 exd5 10 ♘e2 is objectively roughly equal, but Black has a nice position. White's d-pawn is weak, and Black is able to develop with ...c6, ...♗g4, ...♘a6, ...♘c7 and ...♘e6. The

black knight can also move to d7 and then to b6 if White tries a minority attack with b4.

C3)

5 ♘f3

Here we discuss miscellaneous lines where White avoids or delays playing ♘c3.

5...0-0 6 0-0

6 d5?! is premature; d5 is usually only a decent move when White's c-pawn is on c2, so as to meet ...♗b4+ with c3. Black should reply 6...♗b4+! 7 ♘bd2 ♕e7 (Black's plan is simply to play ...e5 and ...d6 and then checkmate White with a timely ...f4, ...♕f7-h5, ...♗h3 and ...♘g4 – you have to dream! The fact that the dark-squared bishop has been developed outside the pawn-structure also benefits Black) 8 ♘d4? (after this error, the game is effectively over) 8...♗c5 9 ♘4b3 ♕xc4 10 0-0 ♕g4 11 h3 ♕h5 12 dxe6 dxe6 13 a3 ♗e7 14 ♘d4 e5 ∓ Annakov-S.Williams, Hastings Challengers 1999/00. Black has an extra pawn and a standard Classical Dutch attack.

6...d6

Now we consider a couple of alternatives to 7 ♘c3 (which is the subject of Chapters 1-3):

C31: 7 b3   58
C32: 7 b4   59

7 ♘bd2 is wrong here since the knight is badly placed on d2; it should almost always go to c3, where it has more control over the central squares. Black can reply 7...♘c6 (now that d5 is not possible, the black knight can

feel confident sitting on c6) 8 b3 e5 with equality.

C31)

7 b3

This move poses no threat to Black since he can now force the ...e5 advance.

7...♘e4! *(D)*

W

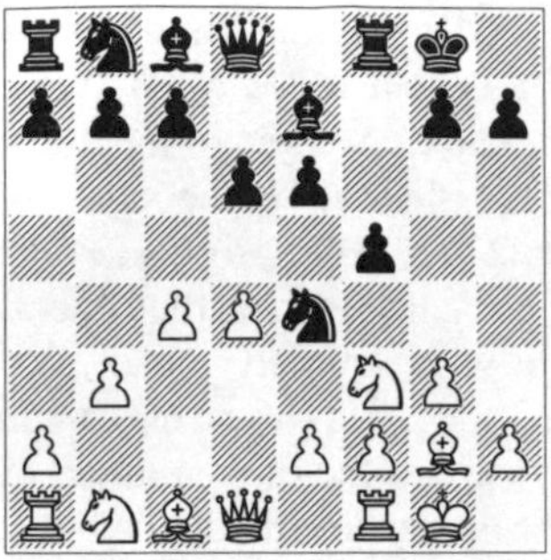

This typical thrust makes room for the e7-bishop to move to f6, and is especially good here, since it takes away the c3-square from White's queen's knight.

8 ♗b2 ♗f6

This is the bishop's rightful home. White now has a choice of two moves:

C311: 9 ♘c3 58
C312: 9 ♘bd2 59

C311)

9 ♘c3 ♘xc3

Another option is 9...♘c6, which I have played myself. This also seems sufficient for equality: 10 ♕c2 ♘xc3 11 ♗xc3 e5 = 12 dxe5 dxe5 13 e4 f4 14 gxf4?! (better is 14 ♕b2 with the idea of playing b4 and b5 but Black is fine after 14...♕e8 15 b4 ♗g4) 14...exf4 (this type of position is often reached in the Classical Dutch – its assessment depends on whether White's fluent centre is more dangerous than Black's kingside attack; here Black's attack is too strong) 15 e5 ♗e7 16 ♕e4 ♗e6 ∓ 17 ♖fd1 ♕e8 18 b4 ♕h5 19 b5 ♘d8 20 ♘d4 ♗c5 21 ♘xe6 ♘xe6 22 ♖d3 ♕h4 23 ♔h1 ♘g5 24 ♕d5+ ♔h8 25 ♕xc5 f3 and Black has a big attack, Mohota-S.Williams, Hastings 2001/2.

10 ♗xc3 ♘c6

This is good now that White can't reply with 11 d5. Black's next move will be 11...e5, getting a slight edge due to his dynamic centre.

11 ♖c1

11 e3 e5 12 dxe5 dxe5 13 ♕d5+ (it is worth noting this move, as it turns up in a lot of positions; Black has nothing to fear since the queen will soon be kicked away) 13...♔h8 14 ♖ad1 (14 ♘xe5?? loses to 14...♕xd5 15 cxd5 ♘xe5 –+) 14...♕e7 ∓ and Black will continue with ...♗e6, booting the queen back home, with a very comfortable position.

11...e5 12 dxe5 dxe5 13 ♕d5+ ♔h8 14 ♕xd8

Otherwise Black plays ...♕e7 and ...♗e6.

14...♖xd8 15 ♖fd1

White's plan is to play ♘e1, ♗xc6 and ♘d3 with pressure against Black's e-pawn.

15...♗e6!

Black can stop White's idea.

16 ♘e1 ♗g5!

Otherwise White will achieve a nice position with the planned 17 ♗xc6 bxc6 18 ♘d3, because if Black moves his e-pawn, White will capture on f6, ruining Black's pawn-structure.

17 ♖b1 e4!

As White can no longer play ♗xf6, Black is doing well.

C312)

9 ♘bd2 ♘c6

As a rule, this is nearly always good as long as White can't reply with d5, since it supports the ...e5 advance and puts pressure on d4. Given a chance, Black will capture on d2 and play ...e5 with equality.

10 ♕c2

White's other sensible options are:

a) 10 ♘xe4 (White's plan is to play a timely f3 breaking up Black's pawn-structure, when White will have a positional superiority) 10...fxe4 11 ♘e1 d5 12 ♘c2 (12 f3? is premature since White's d-pawn will be too weak after 12...dxc4) and now:

a1) 12...♘a5 is a slight error since White can reply with 13 ♗c3!, gaining an advantage. Instead, 13 ♖b1?! b6 14 ♘e3 ♗b7 ∓ was Speelman-S.Williams, British Ch (Millfield) 2000.

a2) Black should play 12...♘e7!. This move makes way for either ...c5 or ...c6, while Black's knight will find a home on f5.

b) 10 ♘e1 and here Black went wrong with 10...♘g5? 11 f4! ± in Speelman-I.Ivanov, Hastings 1983/4 (Black will find it hard to play the ...e5 advance). He should play 10...♘xd2!, which is natural and good. After 11 ♕xd2 e5 = Black has achieved his goal.

10...♘xd2 11 ♕xd2 e5

I like Black's practical chances here since his centre is more fluid. Black's kingside advance is always the more dangerous plan; ...g5-g4 is one idea, when the black queen can go to g7 via e7, with pressure on d4 and the kingside.

12 dxe5 dxe5 13 ♕d5+ ♔h8

The game is equal. White must now avoid 14 ♘xe5?? ♕xd5 15 cxd5 ♘xe5 −+.

C32)

7 b4!? (D)

This is an interesting attempt to grab some space on the queenside; White's plan now is not to play e4 but to try to suffocate Black on the queenside.

7...♘e4

Making way for either the e7-bishop or the b8-knight to move to f6.

Unfortunately, 7...e5?! is bad because of 8 dxe5 dxe5 9 ♘xe5 ♕xd1 (if 9...♗xb4 then 10 ♕b3 ±; Black has too many problems, such as b7 and the a2-g8 diagonal) 10 ♖xd1 ♗xb4 ±. White's pieces are better placed and the pressure against Black's queenside is unpleasant.

8 ♗b2 a5 9 a3

The other option is 9 b5 a4 (the idea behind this pawn push is to hinder the development of White's knight) 10 a3 (if 10 ♘c3? then Black plays 10...a3, and 10 ♘bd2 is also met by 10...a3) and now both 10...♘d7 and 10...c6 look fine for Black, but again there are no practical examples of this.

9...axb4 10 axb4 ♖xa1 11 ♗xa1 (D)

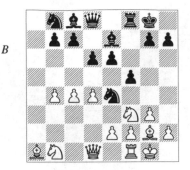

11...b5!?

This interesting move was chosen by the English IM Nick Pert. Black clears the way for ...♗b7 and takes the d5-square. This is a risky approach though, as Black is gambiting a pawn when his position is already solid. Black has two safer ways of playing:

a) 11...♗f6 is a solid approach for Black; he can aim for the ...e5 advance with ...♕e7 and ...♘d7. White has a small space advantage but Black has no weaknesses. Practical examples are needed.

b) 11...♘d7!? is interesting. This leaves the option of playing ...b5 in the air, and the knight can also move to f6 or b6, where it is well placed. Again White has a space advantage but Black has no weaknesses.

12 cxb5 ♘d7 13 d5! (D)

White cannot allow Black to place his d7-knight at d5, as the two knights would then control the whole board. After 13...e5 14 ♘fd2 (Black's pesky knight on e4 needs to be removed) 14...♘xd2 15 ♕xd2 ♘b6 16 ♘c3 ♗d7 17 e3 ♕a8 18 ♗b2 ± Krush-N.Pert, Hastings Premier 2001/2, White has an extra pawn and can infiltrate on the queenside.

Part 2: Classical Dutch with ...♝b4(+)

If White plays an early c4, then Black has the option of playing a line based around ...♝b4(+). The coverage of the ...♝b4(+) lines is divided between two chapters, as follows:

Chapter 5: White avoids fianchetto-ing his king's bishop

Chapter 6: White fianchettoes his king's bishop

1 d4 f5 2 c4 e6 3 g3 ♞f6 4 ♝g2 ♝b4+ (D)

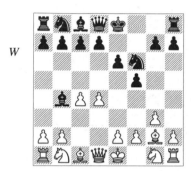

The positions reached after the move ...♝b4(+) are similar but distinctively different from those reached in the Ilyin-Zhenevsky system. When Black plays ...♝e7, he normally intends to place the bishop on f6 at some point. In this line Black often has to give up his dark-squared bishop. In many cases this gives him more space and time to play ...e5, as the e7-square is available to the black queen.

However, Black must remember that White can rule out this line entirely by delaying c4 until he has developed his kingside pieces. Thus 4...♝b4+ should not be the only weapon in Black's arsenal.

5 Classical Dutch with ...♗b4(+): White Avoids Fianchettoing

In this system White avoids fianchettoing and normally places his light-squared bishop on d3. The drawback of this for White is that it gives Black the opportunity to fianchetto his light-squared bishop on b7. The bishop is well placed here as it controls some important central squares, primarily e4. The opening tends to revolve around this square and whether Black can control it, or whether White can successfully play the e4 advance.

Black's Strategy

Black has some ideas which are more effective now that White hasn't fianchettoed his king's bishop. The following plans are worth bearing in mind for Black:

1) As stated above, Black should fianchetto his light-squared bishop by playing ...b6 and ...♗b7. When combined with ...♗b4 and ...♘e4, this offers Black good control over the e4-square.

2) The rook lift ...♖f6-h6 or ...♖f6-g6: on h6 or g6 the rook is well placed for an attack against the white king. Given time, Black can increase the pressure with ...g5, ...g4, ...♕h4 and sometimes ...♗d6. The b7-bishop also adds weight to Black's attack. This plan is more effective for Black when White keeps his dark-squared bishop locked in behind his pawn-structure (i.e. the e3-pawn). The following two games show how dangerous Black's attack can become after this rook manoeuvre:

Lubbers – Bok
Netherlands tt 1985

1 d4 e6 2 c4 b6 3 ♘c3 ♗b4 4 e3 ♗b7 5 ♘f3 f5

Play has transposed to a Classical Dutch.

6 ♗d3 ♘f6 7 0-0 ♗xc3 8 bxc3 0-0 9 a4 ♘e4 10 ♕b3 ♖f6! 11 a5 ♖g6 12 axb6? *(D)*

White is oblivious to Black's kingside threats.

12...♘c5! 13 bxc7 ♖xg2+ 14 ♔h1

If White accepts the rook with 14 ♔xg2, then Black finishes White off with 14...♕g5+ 15 ♔h1 ♗xf3#.

14...♖xh2+ 15 ♔xh2 ♕xc7+ 0-1

White loses his queen.

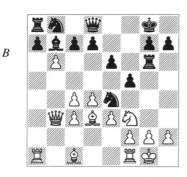

Ylisela – Pyhälä
Finnish Ch (Helsinki) 1987

1 d4 b6 2 c4 e6 3 ♘c3 ♝b4 4 ♘f3 ♝b7 5 e3 f5

Again transposing to a Dutch.

6 ♝d3 ♘f6 7 0-0 ♝xc3 8 bxc3 0-0 9 c5 ♘e4 10 cxb6 axb6 11 ♕c2 ♖f6! 12 ♘e1 ♖h6 *(D)*

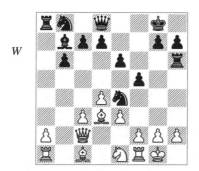

13 f3 ♕h4 14 h3 ♘g5 15 e4 f4 16 ♖f2 ♘c6 17 ♝f1 ♕g3 18 ♔h1 ♖g6 0-1

3) The move ...c5 also regularly figures in Black's plans. ...c5, often combined with ...♘c6, is useful since it puts pressure on the d4-square and in

turn this makes it difficult for White to move his e3-pawn as it is needed to defend the d4-pawn. Another advantage of ...c5 is that Black often swaps off one of White's central pawns for a wing pawn. The next game shows an example of this.

Silman – Moskalenko
Pardubice 1994

1 d4 e6 2 c4 f5 3 ♘f3 ♘f6 4 ♘c3 ♝b4 5 ♕b3 c5!? *(D)*

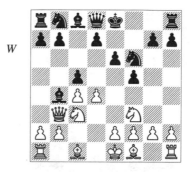

6 dxc5 ♘a6!

Black has already equalized.

7 ♝d2 0-0 8 g3 ♕e7 9 ♝g2 ♘xc5 10 ♕c2 b6 11 0-0 ♝b7 12 ♘d5!? ♝xd5 13 cxd5 ♝xd2 14 ♘xd2 ♖ac8 15 ♖ac1? e5!

Another thematic move from Black.

16 b4 ♘ce4 17 ♕xc8 ♘xd2 18 ♕c7 ♘xf1 19 ♖xf1 ♕xb4 20 ♕xa7 ♕b2

Black has a big advantage.

White's Ideas
As White's bishop is normally placed on d3, Black has to face some new ideas which wouldn't be available to

White in the Ilyin-Zhenevsky System. The two main ones are as follows:

1) The move g4 comes into the equation, since White wishes to open the b1-h7 diagonal for his queen and bishop.

2) The move d5 is much stronger now, because if Black captures ...exd5 White often has the reply ♗xf5 with threats on the b1-h7 diagonal. This is especially the case when Black has played ...d6, as he can no longer recapture on e6 with his d-pawn.

Ippolito – Shabalov
US Open (Alexandria) 1996

1 d4 e6 2 c4 b6 3 ♘f3 ♗b7 4 ♘c3 ♗b4 5 ♕c2 f5 6 ♗g5 ♘f6 7 e3 0-0 8 ♗d3 d6 9 0-0-0 ♗xc3 10 ♕xc3 ♘bd7 11 d5 *(D)*

Opening up the centre to White's advantage.

11...exd5 12 ♗xf5 ♕e8 13 ♗xd7 ♘xd7 14 cxd5 ♘c5

White is better. He is a pawn up and has successfully blocked out Black's b7-bishop. Clearly, the move ...d6 weakened the e6-f5 pawn-chain.

Theory of the Classical Dutch with ...♗b4: White Avoids Fianchettoing

1 d4 f5 2 c4 e6 3 ♘c3 ♘f6

White can now choose from three sensible moves:

A:	4 ♕c2	64
B:	4 ♗g5	66
C:	4 ♘f3	68

A)

4 ♕c2 *(D)*

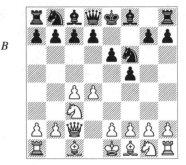

This is the most aggressive square for White's queen. ♕c2 is normally combined with ♗d3 and f3 in order to block out Black's bishop, which usually moves to b7. White often aims to play e4 here, but it is doubtful whether e4 will ever be very effective. Black now has a number of viable replies.

4...♗b4

This looks like the best square for Black's bishop, since it gives him extra control of the e4-square. Black has two other sensible options:

a) 4...b6 (this will more likely than not transpose to 4...♗b4 lines) 5 f3

♗b4 6 ♗g5 ♗b7 7 e3 ♗e7! (it's a good plan for Black to swap off the dark-squared bishops, since White's dark-square weaknesses will begin to show, i.e. e3 and potentially d4) 8 ♗d3 ♘h5 9 ♗xe7 ♕xe7 10 0-0-0 d6 11 ♔b1 g6 12 ♘h3 ♘d7 13 ♖he1 0-0-0 14 e4 f4 15 ♕a4 ♔b8 16 ♘b5 a6 17 ♘c3 c5 18 ♗f1 cxd4 19 ♖xd4 ♘e5 gives Black a slight advantage due to his better control over the dark squares, Slipak-Peralta, Argentine Ch (Pinamar) 2002.

b) 4...♗e7 was played several times by Larsen. The idea is to preserve the dark-squared bishop, and play ...c5. This idea has only been played a dozen times so it may be worth experimenting with it. If White fianchettoes his light-squared bishop, Black can reach an Ilyin-Zhenevsky System but with White's queen already on c2, which is advantageous for Black. White has tried a number of moves here:

b1) 5 e4? is a mistake owing to 5...fxe4 6 ♘xe4 ♘xe4 7 ♕xe4 ♗b4+, when White's king will be misplaced.

b2) 5 ♘f3 0-0 and now:

b21) 6 e4?! doesn't promise White any advantage after 6...fxe4 7 ♘xe4 ♘c6! 8 ♘xf6+ ♗xf6 9 ♗e3 e5! = Pachman-Larsen, Havana OL 1966.

b22) 6 ♗g5 and now Black should make use of his bishop being on e7 and play 6...♘e4! 7 ♗xe7 ♕xe7 with equality, since exchanges benefit Black; he should continue with ...b6 and ...♗b7.

b3) 5 e3 ♘a6!? (an interesting move: Black has ideas of ...♘b4 or ...c5) 6 a3 c5! 7 ♘f3 b6 8 d5 ♗b7 9 dxe6 dxe6 10 b3 0-0 11 ♗b2 ♘c7 12

♗d3 ♕e8 = Sorin-Larsen, San Martin 1995.

5 e3 b6

Black's other decent option is 5...0-0 (transpositions between this and 5...b6 occur frequently) 6 ♗d3 c5 7 ♘ge2 ♘c6 8 0-0 d6 9 a3 ♗xc3 10 ♕xc3 a5! (this is a good move since it prevents White from expanding on the queenside with b4), and then:

a) 11 ♕c2?! gives Black no trouble: 11...♕b6 12 dxc5 dxc5 13 ♘c3 ♘e5 14 ♗e2 ♗d7 15 b3 ♗c6 16 ♗b2 ♘f7 17 ♘b5 ♕d8! 18 ♖ad1 ♕e7 19 f3 b6 = Aleksandrov-Ulybin, Russia Cup (Krasnodar) 1997.

b) 11 b3 is better. White may be able to keep a small advantage after 11...e5 12 dxc5 dxc5 13 ♘g3! e4 14 ♗c2 since his dark-squared bishop will find its ideal home on the a1-h8 diagonal.

6 ♗d3 0-0

Black went straight for the throat in Sirotkina-L.Zaitseva, Russian wom Ch (Elista) 1996, and it paid off: 6...♗b7 7 f3 0-0 8 ♘e2 ♘h5!? 9 0-0 ♕h4 10 ♘b5? a6 11 ♘bc3 ♗d6 12 g3 ♕h3 13 e4 ♘c6 14 e5? ♘xe5! 15 dxe5 ♗c5+ 16 ♖f2 ♗xf2+ 17 ♔xf2 ♕xh2+ 18 ♔e3 ♘xg3 19 ♘f4 ♘f1+ 0-1.

7 ♘e2 ♗b7 8 0-0 ♘c6

The knight plans on moving around to the kingside via e7.

9 f3 ♗d6

An interesting plan: Black's pieces look strangely placed, but he quickly creates play against White's kingside with his bishops.

10 a3 a5

To prevent White from playing b4.

11 ♘b5 ♗e7 12 b3 ♘a7 13 ♘bc3

White should keep pieces on the board since he has more space. Other moves:

a) 13 e4?! ♘xb5 14 cxb5 fxe4 15 fxe4 ♘g4.

b) 13 ♘xa7 ♖xa7 14 e4?! fxe4 15 fxe4 ♘g4 16 ♖xf8+ ♕xf8 17 ♘c3 ♗c5! 18 dxc5 ♕xc5+ 19 ♔f1 ♖a8 followed by 20...♖f8+ gives Black an irresistible attack.

13...♘c8 14 ♗d2

The light-squared bishop will be a useful defender for White's kingside.

14...♔h8 15 ♔h1 c5

Now:

a) 16 ♘a4?! ♗d6 17 b4 axb4 18 axb4 cxd4 19 exd4 (after 19 ♘xd4? ♘g4! 20 h3 ♕h4 Black has a big advantage) 19...♘h5 (Black's bishops are very well placed, staring towards the white king) 20 g3 ♗c7 21 ♖ae1 ♘e7 (bringing another piece into the attack) 22 ♘ac3 ♘g6 23 ♔g1 ♕f6 24 ♖f2 ♖ac8 25 ♕b3 f4 26 g4 ♘g3! gives Black the advantage, Lautier-Vaïsser, French Ch (Marseilles) 2001.

b) The simple 16 ♖fd1 is better. The idea is to play d5 at some point, when White holds a small advantage.

B)

4 ♗g5 (D)

The pin on the f6-knight is quite annoying for Black. However, White normally has to give up his bishop for Black's knight, so Black should obtain equality without too many worries.

4...♗b4!

4...♗e7?! is a slight mistake since it gives White the chance to play e4 at

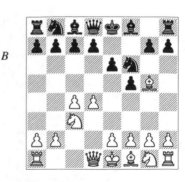

B

some point, after an exchange of minor pieces on f6.

After 4...♗b4! Black's plans include the following:

1) ...d6 followed by ...e5 and ...c5, which is an especially effective idea when White has doubled c-pawns.

2) A quick ...c5 followed by ...♕a5 and, if given the chance, ...♘e4, with pressure against White's c3-knight.

3) Black should combine the above ideas with the simple development of his light-squared bishop by ...b6 and ...♗b7.

White now has a number of options:

B1: 5 e3   67
B2: 5 ♘f3   67
B3: 5 ♕b3   67

There is considerable scope for transpositions to occur. A couple of more minor options:

a) 5 ♖c1 does not cause Black any problems: 5...0-0 6 a3 ♗xc3+ 7 ♖xc3 d6 8 ♘f3 ♘bd7 9 e3 (Penuela-Pena, Barranquilla 1999) and now 9...e5 = is begging to be played.

b) 5 ♕c2 gives Black the chance of attacking White's bishop with 5...h6 (this is not available to Black in the case of 5 ♕b3) 6 ♗xf6 ♕xf6, and now:

b1) 7 a3 ♗xc3+ 8 ♕xc3 d6 9 e3 0-0 10 ♗d3 e5 11 ♘e2 ♘c6 12 0-0-0 ♗d7 = Brinckmann-Ahues, W.German Ch (Bad Pyrmont) 1949. I like Black's practical chances based on his strong centre.

b2) 7 ♘f3 0-0 8 a3 ♗xc3+ 9 ♕xc3 d6 10 e3 b6 (10...♘d7 followed by ...e5 may be an even better plan) 11 ♗e2 ♗b7 12 0-0 ♘d7 13 ♖ac1 (Milić-Kostić, Yugoslav Ch (Ljubljana) 1947) and now 13...e5 = looks fine.

B1)
5 e3
This allows permanent damage to White's pawn-structure.

5...♗xc3+ 6 bxc3 0-0 7 ♗d3 d6 8 ♘e2
8 ♕c2 should not concern Black: 8...♕e8 9 ♘e2 ♘bd7 10 0-0 b6 11 f3 (not 11 e4?! fxe4 12 ♗xe4 ♘xe4 13 ♕xe4 ♗a6!) 11...♕h5 12 ♗xf6 ♖xf6 13 ♘g3 ♕h4 14 ♖f2 ♗b7 15 e4 f4! 16 ♘f1 e5 ∓ Broemel-Knaak, E.German Ch (Stralsund) 1988.

8...e5!
8...c5 is a mistake owing to 9 f4! (Donner-Meulders, Marbella Z 1982), when Black will find it hard ever to play ...e5.

9 0-0 c5 10 ♕b1 h6 11 ♗xf6 ♕xf6 12 a4 ♘c6
Black is slightly better, Khamgo-kov-Naumkin, Moscow 1995.

B2)
5 ♘f3 h6 6 ♗xf6 ♕xf6 7 e3

7 ♕b3 gives Black no problems: 7...♘c6 (7...c5!? appears natural) 8 0-0-0 ♗xc3 9 ♕xc3 d6 10 e3 0-0 11 ♗d3 e5 ½-½ Condie-Mah, British Ch (Swansea) 1995. Black is even a bit better in the final position.

7...0-0
Another good option for Black is 7...d6 8 ♗e2 ♘c6 9 0-0 ♗xc3 10 bxc3 0-0 11 ♘d2 (11 d5 does not help, because White's c-pawns will be very weak after 11...♘e7, while 11...♘a5 is also OK) 11...e5 12 ♖b1 b6 13 f4 exd4 14 exd4 = Moskalenko-Birmingham, Cannes 1990.

8 ♗e2 ♗xc3+ 9 bxc3 d6 10 0-0 ♘c6
Now 11 ♕a4! ♗d7 (in this case 11...e5?! allows White to play 12 c5! dxc5 13 ♕c4+ with an edge) 12 ♕a3 b6 (again 12...e5 runs into 13 c5!, when White has the edge) 13 c5 (Bangiev-Savchenko, Lvov 1988) 13...bxc5 is fine for Black.

B3)
5 ♕b3
This seems to put the most pressure on Black's position, and White also avoids doubled pawns. However, Black has an effective reply.

5...c5! (D)
This is Black's most active answer to 5 ♕b3.

6 a3?!
White gets a bad position after this, but the other options are also not awe-inspiring:

a) 6 dxc5 is yet to be tried, but it doesn't really put any demands on Black's position. Play might continue

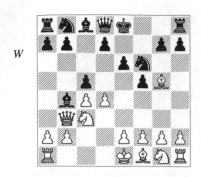

W

6...♘c6 7 e3 ♗xc5 8 ♘f3 0-0 9 ♗e2 ♕a5 =.

b) 6 d5 e5 7 e3 0-0 8 ♗d3 d6 9 ♘ge2 h6 10 ♗xf6 ♕xf6 and Black had a nice edge in Harrwitz-Morphy, Paris 1858.

c) 6 e3 0-0 7 a3 (after 7 ♗d3 Black should play the simple 7...h6 8 ♗xf6 ♕xf6 =) 7...♕a5 8 ♗d3 ♗xc3+ 9 bxc3 ♘c6 (Black has another good option in 9...cxd4!? 10 exd4 ♘e4 11 ♗xe4 fxe4 12 ♗e3 ♘c6, when White's c-pawn will prove to be weak after a subsequent ...♕c7 and ...♘a5) 10 ♘e2 d6 11 0-0 (Chiburdanidze-Yusupov, Linares 1988) and now Black should play 11...e5! with a nice position.

6...♗xc3+ 7 ♕xc3 cxd4 8 ♕xd4 0-0 9 g3 ♘c6 10 ♕c3 d5 11 ♗xf6

If 11 ♗g2 then 11...d4 is strong.

11...♖xf6 12 cxd5 exd5

The simple 12...♕xd5 also retains a slight edge: 13 ♘f3 e5 14 ♗g2 (14 ♖d1 ♘d4) 14...♖d6 with ...e4 to follow; Black controls the d-file.

13 ♗g2 d4 14 ♕c5 ♗e6 15 ♘h3 ♘a5 16 ♘f4 ♗f7 17 ♖d1 ♘b3

Black has a big advantage.

18 ♕e5 ♕d7 19 ♘d5 ♖e6 20 ♕c7 ♖xe2+!!

A brilliant way to break through White's defences.

21 ♔xe2 ♕b5+ 22 ♖d3 ♖e8+

Black has a massive attack, Garcia Palermo-An.Rodriguez, Villa Gesell 1997.

C)

4 ♘f3 (D)

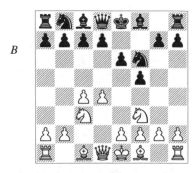

B

Play will often transpose to Line A or B, but there are some independent ideas.

4...♗b4

4...♗e7 will probably transpose to a line looked at elsewhere:

a) 5 g3 0-0 6 ♗g2 d6 7 0-0 is the Ilyin-Zhenevsky System, covered in Chapters 1-3.

b) 5 ♕c2 transposes to note 'b' to Black's 4th move in Line A, which is roughly equal.

c) 5 d5!? is an independent try. After 5...0-0 White has tried two continuations:

c1) 6 e3 ♗b4! 7 ♗d2 ♕e7 8 ♗d3 c6! 9 dxe6 dxe6 10 a3 ♗d6 11 b4 e5 12 c5 ♗c7 13 e4 fxe4 14 ♘xe4 ♘xe4 15 ♗xe4 ♗f5 = Stein-A.Zaitsev, USSR Ch (Moscow) 1969.

c2) 6 g3 ♝b4!; Black wishes to continue with ...♛e7 and ...e5, when he has a nice position.

5 ♝d2

Or:

a) 5 ♝g5 transposes to Line B2.

b) 5 e3 ♝xc3+ is fully satisfactory for Black due to White's crippled pawns and his difficulty in finding an effective role for his queen's bishop.

c) 5 ♛b3 c5 6 dxc5 ♞a6! = Silman – Moskalenko, Pardubice 1994. See the chapter intro for the continuation of this game.

5...0-0

6 e3 *(D)*

6 ♛c2?! is a different plan, but it seems a bit pointless now, since Black is not threatening to double White's pawns any more. 6...c5! (since White has wasted time with ♝d2 and ♛c2, it makes sense to strike out against the centre) 7 e3 ♞c6 8 ♖d1 ♛e7 9 g3 d6 10 ♝g2 cxd4 11 exd4 e5 12 dxe5 dxe5 13

0-0 e4 14 ♞g5 ♞d4 15 ♛b1 ♝xc3 16 bxc3 ♞c6 gives Black an advantage, Bond-Spraggett, Vancouver Keres mem 1986.

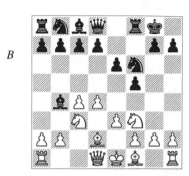

6...b6 7 ♝d3 ♝b7 8 0-0 d6 9 a3 ♝xc3 10 ♝xc3 ♞e4 11 ♞e1 ♞xc3 12 bxc3 ♞d7 13 f3 ♛g5 14 ♛e2 e5 15 f4 exf4 16 exf4 ♛g6 17 ♞f3 ♖ae8 18 ♛c2 ♖e3 19 d5 ♞c5

Black is better due to White's pawn weaknesses, Modr-Hertneck, Dortmund 1988.

6 Classical Dutch with ...♗b4(+): White Fianchettoes

In this line Black can use 4...♗b4+ in two different ways: it can either be used to seek simplifications by exchanging a pair of minor pieces, or it can used to disrupt White's development. Some points to remember when playing this line:

1) After 5 ♘d2 and a later exchange of Black's dark-squared bishop for White's knight, Black has to be wary of playing the pawn advance ...e5, as this allows White to get unchallenged pressure with his bishop on the a1-h8 diagonal.

2) When White plays 5 ♘d2, Black should bear in mind that White has less control over the d5-square, and this might help Black to play ...♘c6 without White being able to reply d5, or Black may be able to fianchetto his light-squared bishop.

3) Unlike the Ilyin-Zhenevsky system, where Black castles before undertaking any action, Black should not be in a rush to castle, as the tempo spent castling can often be used to achieve the ...e5 advance instead.

1 d4 f5 2 c4 e6 3 g3

3 ♘c3 is a natural move when combined with a kingside fianchetto, but it gives Black the added option of playing ...♗b4. For example, 3...♘f6 4 g3 ♗b4 5 ♗d2 (5 ♗g2?! transposes to Line A, and this gives Black a pleasant game) 5...0-0 6 ♗g2 d6 7 ♘f3 ♗xc3 8 ♗xc3 ♘e4 9 ♕c2 ♘d7 10 0-0 and now 10...♘df6?! 11 ♘d2 ♘xc3 12 ♕xc3 transposes to Polugaevsky-Makarychev, Reykjavik 1990. Then 12...e5 13 dxe5 dxe5 14 e4! gave White some advantage, even though Black had achieved the ...e5 advance, since that same pawn proved rather weak. Black should prefer 10...♘xc3 11 ♕xc3 ♕e7 = when he can force the e-pawn to e5 and possibly e4.

3...♘f6 4 ♗g2 ♗b4+

White has answered this check in three different ways:

A: 5 ♘c3?!   70
B: 5 ♗d2   71
C: 5 ♘d2   76

A)

5 ♘c3?! *(D)*

This move merely lets Black double White's c-pawns without any cost.

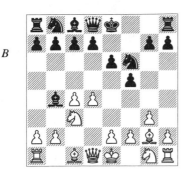

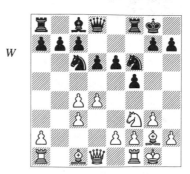

7...0-0 8 0-0 ♘c6 (D)

I consider the position to be equal.

5...♗xc3+

5...0-0 also offers Black an easy game:

a) 6 ♕b3 ♕e7 (the queen is well placed here, supporting the ...e5 advance) 7 a3 ♗xc3+ 8 ♕xc3 d6 9 ♘h3?! (a poor square for the knight) 9...e5 10 dxe5 dxe5 11 0-0 ♘e4 (highlighting the misplaced knight on h3) 12 ♕c2 ♘c6 ∓ P.Gomez-Salov, Oviedo rpd 1993. Black's play here was thematic.

b) 6 ♘f3 ♘e4 = 7 ♕c2 d6 8 0-0 ♗xc3 9 bxc3 ♘d7 10 ♖d1 ♕e8, Hort-Short, Prague 1990. Black will play ...e5 at some point, or continue to control e4 with ...♘df6, with a nice position in either case.

6 bxc3 d6

This move-order is more precise than 6...0-0, which gives White the option of playing 7 c5!?, when he will rid himself of his doubled c-pawns.

7 ♘f3

Other moves are no better:

a) 7 ♘h3?! makes little sense since Black is going to play ...e5 at some point, keeping White's knight stuck on the side-lines.

b) 7 ♖b1 ♘bd7 is equal since 8 ♗xb7?? loses to 8...♖b8 −+.

9 d5

Otherwise Black plays ...e5 with an easy game; for example:

a) 9 ♕c2 e5 10 dxe5 ♘xe5 (the alternative recapture 10...dxe5 is also fine) 11 ♘xe5 dxe5 = Colon-Spassky, San Juan 1969. White's bishop-pair and open files make up for his weak c-pawns, hence the position is about equal.

b) 9 ♗a3 ♖e8 10 ♕c2 e5 11 dxe5 dxe5 12 ♖fd1 ♗d7 = De Winter-Spassky, Lugano OL 1968.

9...♘a5

This variation bears an uncanny resemblance to Line C1 of Chapter 3, where Black is doing fine.

10 dxe6 ♗xe6 11 ♘d4 ♗xc4 12 ♘xf5 ♕d7 13 ♘e3 ♗e6

Black has a solid position, and the game is equal, Beliavsky-Gulko, USSR Cup (Tbilisi) 1976.

B)

5 ♗d2 (D)

Black has two ways of playing the position now: he can exchange on d2

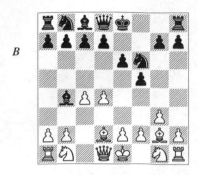

B

at some point and try to achieve the ...e5 break quickly (this is the safer option) or he can retreat the bishop and claim that he has gained something by making White move his bishop to d2.

B1: 5...♕e7   72
B2: 5...♗e7!?   73

The latter idea seems more interesting.

B1)

5...♕e7 (D)

W

White has two sensible moves here:
B11: 6 ♘f3   72
B12: 6 ♘c3   73

B11)

6 ♘f3 ♗xd2+

Black should aim to play ...e5 as soon as possible, and this is why capturing on d2 is more accurate than 6...0-0.

7 ♕xd2

If White plays 7 ♘bxd2 then Black can also respond 7...d6. White's knight is misplaced on d2; it should be on c3, where it exerts more control over the centre. Black can play ...♘c6 next (intending ...e5), since White can no longer reply d5.

7...d6

Black's plan should be apparent to readers by now.

8 ♘c3 e5 (D)

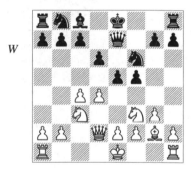

W

9 dxe5

9 0-0 e4 (9...c6 is another good option) is fine for Black. For example, 10 ♘g5 just allows Black to expand on the kingside with 10...h6 11 ♘h3 g5, when 12 f3 allows 12...e3 ∓. After 10 ♘e1 Black can continue with ...c6 and ...d5 at the right moment, maintaining equality.

9...dxe5 10 ♘d5

10 0-0-0 e4 11 ♘d4 0-0 12 f3 ♘c6 13 fxe4 fxe4 14 ♕g5 h6 15 ♘xc6 ½-½ Banikas-Vouldis, Ano Liosia 2000.

Black is doing fine after 15...bxc6; he can even think about starting a queen-side attack with ...♕b4 and ...♖b8.

10...♘xd5 11 cxd5

11 ♕xd5 ♘c6 shouldn't concern Black, as the white queen can quickly be expelled with ...♗e6.

11...e4 12 ♘d4

The position is equal due to White's weakened d-pawn.

12...0-0 13 f3 *(D)*

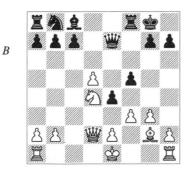

Now, rather than 13...♖d8?! 14 fxe4 fxe4 15 ♘b5 ♕e5 16 ♖d1 c6 17 ♕c3 ♘d7 as in Grabarczyk-Movsesian, Cappelle la Grande 1998, simple development by 13...♘a6! is best. Black then has the preferable position; play might continue 14 ♘c2 exf3 15 ♗xf3 f4, when White's king will become a target. 13...e3!? is another interesting idea; for example, 14 ♕c3 f4.

B12)

6 ♘c3 0-0 7 ♘f3 d6

Another equally effective plan is 7...♗xc3 8 ♗xc3 ♘e4 9 ♖c1 d6 10 0-0 ♘d7 11 ♕b3 ♘df6 12 ♖fd1 b6, when Black has achieved the standard set-up, with his knights controlling the centre

and his bishop well placed on the a8-h1 diagonal. Schandorff-Larsen, Århus 1997 continued 13 ♘d2 ♗b7 14 ♘xe4 ♗xe4 (this is better than 14...♘xe4 since Black wants either to swap off White's good bishop on g2 or to block it out) 15 f3 ♗b7 16 ♕c2 ♖ae8 17 e4 fxe4 18 fxe4 e5 19 d5 ♗c8 =.

8 0-0 ♗xc3 9 ♗xc3 ♘e4 *(D)*

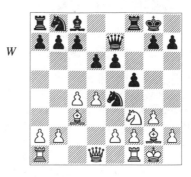

The position is equal. Black plans ...♘d7 and ...♘df6 and, sooner or later, ...e5 gaining precious space in the centre. Orr-D.Johansen, Novi Sad OL 1990 continued 10 ♕e1 (this seems a bit strange; better is 10 ♕c2 or 10 ♖c1) 10...♘d7 11 e3 b6 12 ♘d2 ♗b7 13 ♖c1 c5! (Black is in control of the centre so he decides to gain more space; this useful move also prevents White from ever playing c5 and creating a half-open c-file) 14 b3 ♘df6 15 ♗b2 ♖ad8 16 f3 ♘xd2 17 ♕xd2 e5 ∓.

B2)

5...♗e7!? *(D)*

Black wants to reach a normal Classical position, hoping that the bishop will prove misplaced on d2. The logic is that the d2-bishop gets in the way of

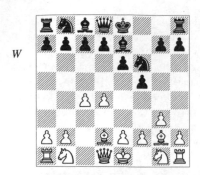

the queen, and so leaves d4 less well covered; the bishop might also be hit by a later ...♞e4.

6 ♞c3

White's queen thrust 6 ♛b3 is a bit premature due to 6...c6! 7 d5 cxd5 8 cxd5 e5! (the difference between this and Line B21 is that White can't play d6+ winning the black bishop, so Black is guaranteed an easy game) 9 ♞f3 d6 =.

6...0-0

White has various options available to him here:

B21: 7 ♛b3 74
B22: 7 ♛c2 75
B23: 7 ♞f3 75

Other moves:

a) 7 ♞h3?! (on h3 this knight is going to be stuck out of the game) 7...d6! 8 0-0 e5 =. Black has got the ...e5 advance in and White's h3-knight is looking rather lost.

b) 7 d5 e5 8 e4 d6 gives Black easy equality; for example, 9 ♛c2 ♞a6 10 exf5 e4! 11 ♞xe4 ♝xf5 12 ♞e2 ♞xe4 13 ♝xe4 ♝xe4 14 ♛xe4 ♝f6 15 0-0 = Rogozenko-Marin, Romanian Ch (Iasi) 1999.

B21)
7 ♛b3

White's queen is quite well placed here, where it eyes the black king on the a2-g8 diagonal, and deters the plan of ...b6 and ...♝b7.

7...c6

This is a safe move that gives Black an easy game. 7...c5!? is riskier since it involves a pawn sacrifice but it is an active alternative, and may find favour with especially aggressive players. 8 d5 (8 dxc5? ♞a6 is good for Black) 8...e5 9 e4 (if 9 d6? then Black is better after 9...♝xd6 10 ♝xb7 ♝xb7 11 ♛xb7 ♞c6 ∓) 9...d6 10 exf5 ♝xf5! (Black has to play actively to prevent White from getting a hold on e4) 11 ♛xb7 ♞bd7 12 ♛a6 (if 12 ♞ge2 then Black gets ample compensation after 12...♜b8 13 ♛xa7 ♜xb2 14 ♛a3 ♛b6) 12...♝d3 13 ♞ge2 ♛e8 and now:

a) 14 b3?! ♛f7 15 0-0 ♛h5 16 f3 g5 17 ♜ae1 e4 18 fxe4 ♞g4 19 h3 ♞de5 with a strong attack and full compensation, Najdorf-Tartakower, Groningen 1946. Any Dutch player should enjoy playing games like this!

b) 14 ♞c1 is better. Black has some compensation after 14...♛g6, but it is not clear if it is sufficient.

8 d5 ♞a6!

This may be Black's best move: he gains a tempo by developing the knight to c5, where it attacks White's queen. There is another option which also looks OK for Black: 8...d6 (it is worth noting that 8...e5?? loses to 9 d6 ♝xd6 10 c5+ +−, and 8...cxd5? 9 cxd5 e5?? to 10 d6+ +−) 9 dxe6 ♞a6 10 ♞h3 ♞c5 11 ♛c2 ♞g4!? 12 0-0 a5 13 b3

♗xe6 (White has the superior pawn-structure, but Black is solid) 14 ♘f4 ♗d7 15 ♘d3 ♘e6 (Black's play is on the kingside) 16 e3 (M.Gurevich-Dolmatov, USSR Ch (Minsk) 1987) and now Black should play 16...♕e8, when he can re-route the e7-bishop to c7, with roughly equal chances.

9 ♘f3 ♘c5 10 ♕c2 ♘ce4 *(D)*

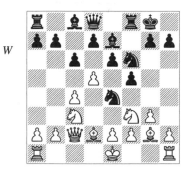

11 dxe6

If 11 ♘d4 then 11...♗c5! is good for Black.

11...♘xd2 12 ♕xd2 dxe6

= Stoll-Perlo, corr. 1989.

B22)

7 ♕c2

This seems to be a logical move: White wishes to play e4 next move, gaining a nice position.

7...d5

The Stonewall structure is justified now since White does not want his bishop to be on d2; in the Stonewall it is much better placed on the a1-h8 diagonal. White's knight is also misplaced on c3; in the Stonewall it is better on d2, where it can move to f3 and then e5.

8 ♘f3 c6 9 0-0 ♕e8! *(D)*

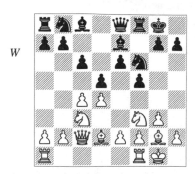

I like this idea: since White's pieces are slightly misplaced, Black transfers his queen to the kingside, where it can help in an assault on the white king. H.Steiner-Botvinnik, Groningen 1946 continued 10 ♗f4 (10 ♗g5 gives Black no problems; he can continue 10...♕h5 11 ♗xf6 ♗xf6 12 cxd5 cxd5 with equality) 10...♕h5 11 ♖ae1 ♘bd7 12 ♘d2? (this allows Black to swap off White's strong dark-squared bishop) 12...g5 13 ♗c7 ♘e8 14 ♗e5 ♘xe5 15 dxe5 f4 ∓; Black has got his kingside play moving.

B23)

7 ♘f3

White sensibly continues developing. Black now two perfectly viable plans:

7...d6!?

This is an interesting plan: Black reaches a kind of Ilyin-Zhenevsky position, but with White's bishop on d2, and this difference seems to favour Black. However, the second option, 7...♘e4 8 0-0 ♗f6, is much more common. Then:

a) 9 ♘xe4? (White should keep the central tension) 9...fxe4 and here:

a1) 10 ♘e5 d6 11 ♘g4 ♗xd4 12 ♗xe4 e5 13 ♘e3 ♘d7 and Black's strong centre gives him an advantage, Nogueiras-Murei, Lucerne OL 1982.

a2) 10 ♘e1 ♗xd4 11 ♗xe4 ♗xb2 12 ♗xh7+ ♔xh7 13 ♕c2+ ♔g8 14 ♕xb2 ♘c6 ∓ Euwe-Alekhine, Delft Wch (24) 1935. Black has the better pawn-structure, and White's c4-pawn is looking very weak.

b) 9 ♕c2 is more thematic. Black now has two options:

b1) 9...♘xd2 (keeping the position in the realms of the Classical Dutch) 10 ♕xd2 d6 11 e4 and now Black should continue 11...e5! =, and not 11...fxe4?, which is a typical mistake and gives White a nice advantage after 12 ♘xe4 ±.

b2) 9...d5 (aiming for a Stonewall set-up) 10 cxd5 exd5 11 ♗f4 c6 12 ♖ad1 ♘d7 13 ♘e1 ♕e7 14 ♘xe4 fxe4 15 b3 = S.Rubinstein-Opočensky, Vienna 1936. Black is no worse thanks to his strong central pawn-formation, which is a good basis for a kingside attack. White should try to break this formation down with f3. If anyone has won the opening battle then it is Black.

8 0-0 (D)

8...♘c6!?

This is a very interesting new idea, trying to benefit from White having his bishop on d2; we shall soon see why this helps Black.

8...♕e8 is another option; e.g., 9 ♕c2 ♕h5 10 e4 e5 11 dxe5 dxe5 12 ♘d5 ♘xd5 13 exd5 ♗f6 = Szabo-Bronstein, Budapest Ct 1950.

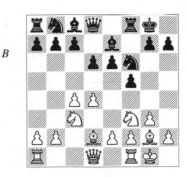

9 d5 ♘e5 10 ♘d4 ♘xc4 11 ♘xe6

11 dxe6 leads to equality: 11...c5 12 ♘xf5 ♗xe6 =.

11...♗xe6 12 dxe6 c6

Now White can't play ♕d3, which is the critical move in the analogous line where White's bishop is on c1 instead of d2 (i.e. line 'b' in the note on 7...♘c6?! at the end of the Part 1 Introduction). The b2-pawn is also attacked. Obviously these factors favour Black; he is slightly better.

It seems to me that in the lines after both 7...♘e4 and 7...d6!? White does not want his bishop to be on d2, he would rather it were back home on c1, out of trouble.

C)

5 ♘d2

White's intention is to force Black to exchange on d2, when he will have the advantage of the bishop-pair.

5...a5 (D)

This is a useful move since it prevents White from expanding with a3 and b4, but the main reason for playing ...a5 is to develop the light-squared bishop on b7 at some point after White plays ♘f3 (we shall see this idea in

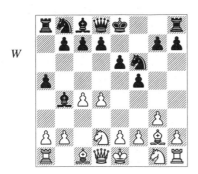

W

Line C3). This continuation is more accurate than castling straight away. Black's priorities should be developing the c8-bishop and then playing the ...e5 break.

White has a number of moves to pick from here:

C1: 6 a3   77
C2: 6 ♘h3!?   77
C3: 6 ♘f3   78

C1)

6 a3

This is not really necessary since Black will probably have to capture on d2 at some point anyway.

6...♝xd2+ 7 ♝xd2 0-0

7...d6 may be more accurate as the fight for e5 is more important than castling. There have been no practical examples of this move yet.

8 ♖c1 ♕e8

Again, Black should consider 8...d6, since this is a move he cannot do without, and it may be better to play it here, so as to wait and see where to place the black queen.

9 c5 d6 10 cxd6 cxd6 11 ♘f3 ♘c6

Black can also consider 11...♕b5, aiming to control some squares on the queenside and planning ...a4 with a grip on b3. Without a c-pawn, White has less control over the centre and Black no longer has to fear d5, but in return White does have the c-file.

12 0-0 (D)

B

12...e5

Black controls the centre, but White has the bishop-pair and more open lines to work on. Another move worth considering for Black is 12...a4!? 13 b3 axb3 14 ♕xb3 ♘e4, when White's a-pawn is weak.

13 ♕b3+ ♔h8!

13...♝e6?! 14 ♕xb7 ♝d5 15 ♘xe5! ♝xg2 16 ♔xg2 ♘xd4 17 ♘f3 ± favours White.

14 d5 ♘e7

The position is equal, Khenkin-Conquest, British League (4NCL) 2000/1.

C2)

6 ♘h3!?

This makes more sense now that Black has played ...♝b4 and ...a5, because if Black continues with ...d6 and ...e5 the b4-bishop is lacking squares and so will have to be exchanged for the d2-knight.

6...♘c6

This is a sensible developing move, but Black has another sound option in the form of 6...d6, which in fact seems more natural since ...♘c6 will always be an option. 7 0-0 ♗xd2 (Black should exchange on d2 before White gets a chance to move his knight from d2, when he would threaten to win Black's b4-bishop by playing a3) 8 ♗xd2 0-0 9 ♖c1 and now:

a) 9...♕e7 10 c5 (this is White's best attempt at claiming an advantage; 10 ♕c2 ♘c6 11 d5 ♘b4 12 ♗xb4 axb4 13 dxe6 c5 gave White nothing in Bottino-Sclortino, Porto San Giorgio 2001) and now Black should play 10...♘e4 with a roughly equal game. 10...♘c6!? is interesting but may not be entirely sound; for example, 11 cxd6 cxd6 12 ♗xc6 bxc6 13 ♖xc6 ♗b7 gives Black some compensation for the pawn, but White can easily block the a8-h1 diagonal with f3.

b) 9...e5! is best, and gives Black a roughly equal game.

7 d5 ♘e5 8 ♕c2 c6 *(D)*

This is an improvement over 8...a4, which was played in Neverov-Conquest, Hastings 1991/2.

Another option is 8...♘f7 with the idea of playing ...e5.

Black needs to create more space for his pieces, and with the text-move he tries to break down White's centre.

9 dxe6

9 ♘f4 may be better. Then Black should probably continue 9...♘f7 with 10...e5 to follow, when the position is unclear.

9...dxe6 10 a3 ♗e7

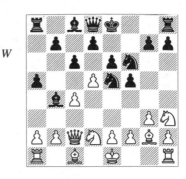

Black needs to keep this bishop now. If it is exchanged for White's knight, the dark squares, especially f4, e5, d6 and c5, would be too weak.

11 b3 ♘f7

Black's plan as always is to play ...e5. On f7 the knight does a good job consolidating the centre and kingside.

12 ♗b2 e5

Black is at least equal, since he has control of the centre while White's knight looks rather stupid on h3.

C3)

6 ♘f3 b6! *(D)*

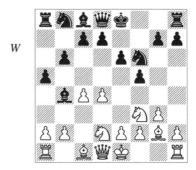

This is the main idea behind ...a5; after White moves his f3-knight, Black can simply play ...♖a7.

7 ♘e5 ♖a7 8 0-0 ♗b7! *(D)*

I believe this move equalizes. The exchange of bishops favours Black, as it is often very difficult for him to find a good square for his c8-bishop, but here he can get rid of it. The g2-bishop helps White play e4 and also exerts pressure against Black's queenside in many positions. It is very surprising that there are no games with this move in MegaBase 2001, which shows how many unexplored positions there are in the Dutch. Other options:

a) 8...0-0?! is inaccurate:

a1) 9 ♘df3?! (missing his chance to get an advantage) 9...♗e7 10 b3 a4 11 ♗d2 ♘e4 = 12 b4 d6 13 ♘d3 ♗f6 14 b5 c5! (opening up the c-file for Black's rooks) 15 bxc6 ♘xc6 16 ♘b4 ♘a5 17 e3 ♗d7 18 ♕e2 ♕c8 19 ♖fc1 ♖c7 ∓ Levitt-N.Pert, Oakham 2001. Black has played thematically and has a nice position due to his c-file pressure and superior minor pieces.

a2) White should play 9 ♘b1! ±, after which Black's bishop will have to retreat. White can then move his b1-knight to c3 at a later stage, and this is a much better square than d2.

b) 8...♗xd2 9 ♕xd2 (White wants to play b3 and ♗b2) 9...d6 =. Black has nothing to fear; his plan is to continue ...♗b7 and ...e5.

W

9 ♘df3

This will tend to lead to the sort of position seen in Levitt-N.Pert (line 'a1' of the previous note), where Black is doing fine. Black's plan is to play ...♗e7 and ...0-0, and then to move forward in the centre at the right time with ...d6, ...♘e4, ...♗f6, ...♘bd7 and eventually ...e5.

7 Alekhine's Variation: 6...♘e4!?

1 d4 f5 2 c4 e6 3 ♘f3 ♘f6 4 g3 ♗e7 5 ♗g2 0-0 6 0-0 ♘e4!? *(D)*

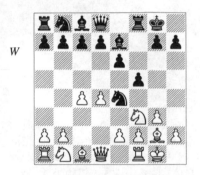

W

6...♘e4!? is an interesting idea. Black keeps the position fluid and retains plenty of options about the future course of the game. Alekhine's Variation doesn't really have one specific strategy but tends to borrow from many different Dutch set-ups, including the Stonewall: Black still has the option of playing ...d5 in one move, which can be useful after an exchange of knights on e4. This flexibility comes at a price though: Black has to be willing to play a wide range of positions, some of which might not be to his taste. For example, a Classical Dutch player might not want to enter a Stonewall set-up but he may be forced to, in order to prevent White from playing e4. Black's

queenside is for the moment undeveloped, but this also has a positive side: it leaves Black more options about where to place these pieces, and he can tailor his set-up according to what White chooses to play.

Here are a couple of things to remember when playing this line:

1) Black should nearly always develop his dark-squared bishop to f6, where it pre-empts White from playing b3 and generally exerts pressure on the a1-h8 diagonal.

2) Black should not swap his e4-knight for a white knight if it allows White to play e4.

After 6...♘e4, White has a number of moves:

A:	**7 d5**	81
B:	**7 ♘c3**	82
C:	**7 ♕c2**	83
D:	**7 ♘bd2**	84

The last is the most demanding on Black's position.

Other moves:

a) 7 b3 gives Black an easy game after 7...♗f6 8 ♗b2 d6, since he has obtained a good version of a Classical line where White can't prevent Black from playing ...e5.

b) 7 ♘fd2 (this seems odd given that White can play ♘bd2) 7...♘xd2 and here:

b1) 8 ♕xd2 d6 9 ♘c3 and now 9...e5 seems equal to me. There have been no examples of this but Black should have no problems. Another decent option for Black is 9...c6 10 e4 e5 11 dxe5 dxe5 12 exf5 ♗xf5 13 ♘e4 ♕c7 =.

b2) 8 ♘xd2 ♗f6 9 e3 d6 =.

b3) 8 ♗xd2 d6 (8...♗f6 9 ♗c3 d5 leaves White's bishop poorly placed on c3 since the d4-pawn blocks its view; in the Stonewall structure it is much better on the c1-h6 diagonal where it can come to f4) 9 e4 ♘c6 (9...e5 may be more accurate) 10 ♗e3 (10 d5 is met by 10...♘e5) 10...e5 = Pötsch-H.Schwarz, Bavaria 1998.

A)

7 d5 (D)

B

White gains space in the centre but opens the a1-h8 diagonal for Black's bishop, and leaves the c5-square available to a black knight.

7...♗f6 8 ♕c2
Other moves:

a) 8 ♘d4?! c5! 9 ♘c2 ♘d6 (the f6-bishop exerts a lot of pressure on the a1-h8 diagonal) 10 dxe6 dxe6 11 ♕d3 ♘c6 12 f4 ♕c7 13 ♘ba3 ♖d8 is slightly better for Black, Simonović-Kostić, Zagreb 1946. White's pieces are clumsily placed, whereas Black's control a lot of important squares.

b) 8 ♘fd2 ♘xd2 9 ♘xd2 e5 (again, as soon as Black plays ...e5 his chances are to be preferred) 10 e4 f4 ∓ O.Kozlov-Poluliakhov, Kobanya 1992.

8...♘a6

Black does have another good option: 8...a5 9 ♘bd2 ♘xd2 (another interesting idea is 9...♘c5!?, keeping more pieces on the board) 10 ♗xd2 d6 (10...e5 also looks OK for Black) 11 dxe6 (White can try 11 e4 fxe4 12 ♕xe4 but after 12...♘a6 Black is fine; 12...e5 is also OK) 11...♗xe6 12 ♖fd1 ♘c6 13 e3 ♕e7 14 ♗c3 ♖ae8 = Ionescu-Bischoff, Lucerne Wcht 1985.

9 ♘fd2
Other moves:

a) 9 ♘c3?! ♗xc3 10 bxc3 just cripples White's pawns; Black can count on an advantage.

b) 9 ♘e1?! (too passive) 9...♘b4 10 ♕d1 a5 11 f3 ♘c5 12 ♘c3 d6 13 ♖b1 c6 14 e4 exd5 15 exd5 cxd5 16 cxd5 ♖e8 17 a3 ♕b6 18 ♔h1 ♕a6!? leaves Black better due to his active pieces, Huerta-Nogueiras, Santa Clara 1980.

c) 9 a3 d6 10 dxe6 ♘ac5 11 ♗e3 ♘xe6 (11...♗xe6 is also equal) 12 ♖d1 ♗d7 13 ♘bd2 ♕e8 = Rogozenko-Haub, Pardubice 1999.

9...♘xd2 10 ♗xd2 d6 11 ♗c3 ♗xc3 12 ♘xc3 e5 13 a3 ♕e8 (D)

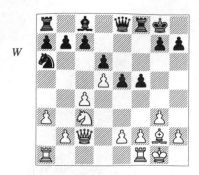

W

The game is equal. Engqvist-R.Bellin, Gausdal 1990 continued 14 b4 ♗d7 15 c5!? dxc5 16 b5 (16 d6 c6 17 bxc5 ♘xc5 18 ♘d5 may be an improvement, but Black is still equal) 16...♘b8 17 d6 c6 18 ♘a4 b6 19 ♘c3 e4 ∓.

B)

7 ♘c3 (D)

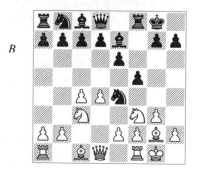

B

7...♗f6

Other moves are bad for Black. For example, 7...♘xc3?! 8 bxc3 d6 is different from lines in Chapter 3 (most notably Line C1) since White has not yet committed his queen. Therefore, instead of playing ♕c2 to prepare e4, he can play 9 ♖e1! ±. Black can try to

meet this with ...e5, but he will simply lose a pawn: 9...♘c6 10 e4! e5 11 exf5 ♗xf5 12 dxe5 (this is why the rook is so good on e1: it also puts pressure on e5) 12...dxe5 13 ♕d5+ ♖f7 14 ♘xe5 ± Tukmakov-Gerber, Lenk 1999.

8 ♕c2

This is White's most natural move. Alternatively:

a) 8 ♘xe4 transposes to note 'd' to White's 8th move in Line D.

b) 8 ♕d3 ♘xc3 (again 8...d5 is an option) 9 bxc3 ♘c6 10 e4 fxe4 11 ♕xe4 transposes to the main line.

c) 8 ♕b3?! (it seems a bit risky for White to leave Black's knight on e4) 8...♘c6 9 ♗e3 b6 10 ♘xe4 fxe4 11 ♘d2 ♗xd4 = 12 ♗xe4 ♗xe3 13 ♕xe3 ♗b7 14 ♖ad1 ♘a5 15 b4 ♗xe4 16 ♕xe4 ♘c6 17 b5 ♘a5 led to a draw in Tartakower-Opočenský, Buenos Aires OL 1939. White's queenside pawns are a target but he has more space.

8...♘xc3

8...d5 is also playable, and gives Black a slightly improved Stonewall due to White having his knight placed on c3. Black still has the option of playing ...♘c6 as well.

9 bxc3 ♘c6

9...d5? is a mistake when White has already recaptured with bxc3 because after the sequence cxd5 exd5 White always has the option of playing c4 again, eliminating Black's only remaining central pawn.

10 e4 fxe4 11 ♕xe4 (D)

The difference between this position and most positions where White plays e4 is that Black has not weakened his e6-pawn with ...d6. White

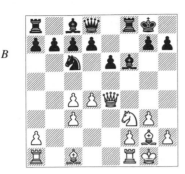

B

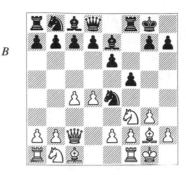

B

also has doubled c-pawns, which will become a target for Black's pieces. Both these factors clearly help Black, so the position is about equal.

11...b6 12 d5 ♘a5 13 c5

13 dxe6 ♗b7 14 ♕g4 dxe6 15 ♕xe6+ ♔h8 ∓ is fine for Black; White has too many weak pawns and Black's pieces are better placed.

13...♔h8?!

This move seems a bit over-cautious; better is 13...♗a6 14 ♖d1 ♗xc3 (or 14...♕e7).

14 ♘e5 bxc5 15 dxe6 ♗b7 16 ♕e2 ♗xg2 17 ♔xg2 dxe6 18 ♖d1 ♕e8 19 ♗f4 ♘c6

½-½ Rashkovsky-Makarychev, Tashkent 1987.

C)

7 ♕c2 (D)

7...♗f6

Other moves appear inferior:

a) 7...d6?! is inaccurate, and should be met by 8 ♘bd2 (8 ♘c3 transposes to Line C of Chapter 3), when play might continue 8...♘xd2 9 ♗xd2 ♗f6 10 e4! ±.

b) 7...♘c6?! is an interesting idea, by which Black is trying to profit from White moving his queen to c2. However, there are only a few examples of this idea:

b1) 8 d5?! ♘b4 9 ♕b3 (if 9 ♕d1 then 9...♗f6 =) and now:

b11) 9...♘a6?! 10 dxe6?! (relieving the tension too soon) 10...dxe6 11 ♖d1 ♕e8 12 ♘c3 ♘ac5 13 ♕c2 ♘xc3 14 ♕xc3 ♗f6 15 ♕c2 ∓ gave Black good play in Haas-Sauer, Germany 1999.

b12) 9...b5! 10 cxb5 ♘xd5 ∓. Black has the better centre.

b2) 8 ♘c3! ♘b4!? (or 8...♘xc3 9 ♕xc3 ±) 9 ♕b1 d6 10 ♘xe4 fxe4 11 ♕xe4 e5 12 dxe5! (more testing than 12 ♕b1? ♗f5 13 e4 ♗g4 14 ♗d2 ♗xf3 15 ♗xb4 exd4 16 ♕d3 ♗h5 ∓ Ferreira-Asmundsson, Buenos Aires OL 1978) 12...♗f5 13 ♕xb7 ± gives White too many extra pawns, and his queen cannot be trapped.

8 ♘c3 d5

Now we have a Stonewall structure, but where Black has not yet played ...c6. This gives him the option of playing ...♘c6 and even ...c5. Also after ...b6 and ...♗b7 the bishop has a better view along the a8-h1 diagonal.

9 ♗f4

After 9 e3 b6 Black should continue with ...♗b7 and ...c5 at the right moment.

9...c6

9...♘c6 is another idea, leading the game in a different direction.

10 ♖ab1 ♘d7 11 ♖fd1 g5 12 ♗c1 ♕e7 13 b4 a6 14 ♘e1 ♘d6 *(D)*

15 c5 ♘b5 16 ♘xb5 axb5

Black is a little better, Lalić-Spraggett, Zaragoza 1996.

D)

7 ♘bd2 *(D)*

This is White's best; it is a good idea for him to swap off Black's strong knight as soon as possible.

7...♗f6 8 ♕c2

Again White's best move: he puts the question to Black's knight straight away. However, he has a number of other possibilities:

a) 8 ♕b3 (the queen is less well placed here, since it exerts no pressure on Black's e4-knight) 8...d6 (this is a new move I am suggesting; as usual, Black plans to play ...e5 at the right moment, and White will have to waste time defending the d4-pawn) 9 e3 ♘xd2 (or else White might play ♘xe4 himself) 10 ♗xd2 ♘d7 = with ...♔h8, ...♕e7 and ...e5 to follow.

b) 8 e3 d6 and here:

b1) 9 ♕c2 offers White no advantage; for example, 9...♘xd2 10 ♗xd2 e5 = 11 dxe5 dxe5 12 ♗b4 ♖f7 13 ♖ad1 ♕e8 14 ♘d2 ♘c6 15 ♗c3 e4! ∓. This is a common theme when the white knight can't jump into d4 immediately. Black gains space, blocks in the g2-bishop and gives his pieces the e5-square.

b2) 9 ♘xe4 fxe4 10 ♘e1 d5 and now Black will have two ways to strike out at White's centre: either ...dxc4 and ...c5 or ...b6 and ...♗b7. In both cases the position will be about equal.

c) 8 b3 ♘c6 (another interesting idea is 8...c5!?, which has only been played once: 9 ♗b2 ♘c6 10 e3 d5 11 cxd5 exd5 12 ♘e5 ♗xe5 13 dxe5 ♗e6 14 f3 ♘xd2 ∓ K.Kuznetsov-M.Heidenfeld, Dubai 2001) 9 ♗b2 d6 transposes to Line C312 of Chapter 4.

d) 8 ♘xe4 fxe4 9 ♘e5 d5 (Black is also OK after 9...c5!?) 10 f3 (10 ♘g4 does not give White anything either; for example, 10...♗e7 11 b3 c5 12

♗b2 ♞c6 13 dxc5 ♗xc5 14 ♞e5 ♛d6 = Bagirov-Gulko, Tbilisi 1978) 10...c5 11 ♗e3 ♗xe5 12 dxe5 d4 13 ♗c1 ♞c6 and Black is slightly better, Vaganian-Bronstein, Leningrad 1971.

8...d5 *(D)*

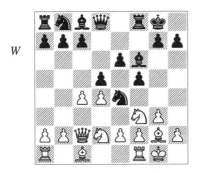

W

9 b3

Other moves give Black an easy game:

a) 9 cxd5?! (releasing the tension so soon like this generally doesn't give White any advantage in this Stonewall structure) 9...exd5 10 b4 ♞c6 11 ♛b2 = Garcia Palermo-Bischoff, Dortmund 1985.

b) 9 ♞e5 ♞d7 10 ♞df3 ♞xe5 11 dxe5 ♗e7 12 ♞e1 c6 13 ♞d3 = B.Jansson-Pytel, Skopje OL 1972. Black is fine due to White's weak pawn on e5; Black can with continue with ...b6 and ...♗b7.

9...c5

Another plan for Black is 9...♞c6 10 ♗b2 a5:

a) 11 cxd5?! (again, this releases the tension too quickly) 11...exd5 12 ♞e5 ♞b4 13 ♛d1 c6 14 ♞df3 ♖e8 15

a3 ♞a6 16 ♛c2 ♞c7 = K.Göhring-Bischoff, Bundesliga 1985/6. Black has a comfortable position.

b) Better is 11 e3 ♗d7 12 a3 ♗e8, when we have a strange Stonewall position that is hard to assess.

10 ♗b2

Other moves don't promise White anything either. For example, 10 ♗a3 can simply be met by 10...♛a5, asking the bishop why it moved there in the first place, while 10 cxd5 ♛xd5 gives Black pressure against White's centre.

10...cxd4 11 ♗xd4

Black's f6-bishop controls some nice central squares (i.e. d4 and e5), so it is a good idea for White to exchange it off. Instead, 11 ♞xd4 led to dull equality in Fine-Alekhine, Amsterdam 1936: 11...♞c6 12 ♞xe4 fxe4 13 ♖ad1 ♛b6 14 ♛d2 ♗d7 15 ♞xc6 ♗xc6 =.

11...♞c6 12 ♗xf6 ♛xf6 13 cxd5 exd5 14 a3 a5

This prevents White's plan of playing b4, ♞b3 and ♞bd4, when he would have the advantage due to his control of the centre, and successful blockade of the d-pawn.

15 ♛d3 ♗e6 16 e3 ♖ad8 17 ♖fd1 ♗f7

I believe this position is equal. Black has an isolated pawn but his pieces are active and he has a stronghold on e4. One plan is ...♗h5 and ...♞e5. Ree-Bronstein, Budapest 1977 continued 18 ♞d4 (it is not easy to see another plan for White) 18...♞e5 19 ♞xe4 fxe4 20 ♛b5 b6 21 ♖ac1 ♞d3 22 ♖c2 ♖c8 ∓.

8 The Staunton and Other Gambits after 1 d4 f5

There are a number of gambits that White can play against the Dutch. Although none of them should pose a serious threat if Black is well prepared, if Black plays inaccurately he can find himself in a lost position very quickly.

The Staunton Gambit is the most popular and dangerous of these gambits. White believes that he can expose the weaknesses of Black's first move by giving up a central pawn with the idea of developing rapidly and starting an attack against Black's king. The positions reached are double-edged, and this should suit a Classical Dutch player. As in most gambits, Black should normally return the pawn at some point so as to wrest the initiative from White.

1 d4 f5

White has a range of gambits available to him here:

A: 2 g4?!	86
B: 2 c4 e6 3 e4?!	87
C: 2 ♘f3 e6 3 e4!?	87
D: 2 e4	88

A)

2 g4?! (D)

Premature aggression. White wants to follow up with h3 and open up lines

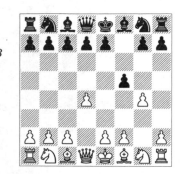

against Black's kingside. However, a better version of the idea is to play h3 first, as shown in Chapter 9, Line A2.

2...fxg4 3 h3

Other moves:

a) 3 e4 e5! 4 dxe5 (4 ♕xg4 runs into 4...♘f6) 4...♘c6 5 ♕xg4 d6 6 ♕g5 ♕xg5 7 ♗xg5 ♘xe5 = Kozlovskaya-Prudnikova, Riazan 1992.

b) 3 ♗f4 (the idea is to stop ...g3 after h3 but this is hardly dangerous) 3...♘f6 4 h3 d5 5 ♘c3 ♘c6 (Black returns the pawn but activates his pieces, and now is in no danger of being mated; he can also play 5...g6, or, if he is feeling brave, 5...gxh3, which can't be that worrying) 6 ♘b5 (the only move) 6...e5 7 ♗xe5 (7 dxe5 is answered by 7...♘h5 =) 7...♗b4+ 8 c3 ♗a5 =.

3...g3!

After this move it is White's king-side that is looking rather exposed.

4 fxg3 ♘f6 5 ♘c3 d5

This is a sensible way of playing. The only structural asymmetry is due to the pawns on h3 and g3; the weakening of White's kingside outweighs the fact that he can develop his king's bishop more quickly. After 6 ♗g2 e6 7 ♘f3 ♗d6! 8 ♘e5 c5 9 ♗f4 ♘h5 10 0-0 0-0 (once White's dark-squared bishop has been eliminated, his position should fall apart) 11 e3 ♘xf4 12 exf4 ♘c6 13 ♘xc6 bxc6 14 ♔h2 ♗a6 15 ♖e1 ♕f6 16 dxc5 ♗xc5 and Black's central pawn majority and bishop-pair ensured him a lasting, albeit slight, advantage in Tregubov-Malaniuk, Linares 1996.

B)

2 c4 e6 3 e4?! *(D)*

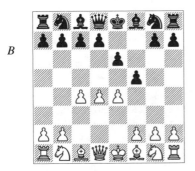

This is over-optimistic. If White wishes to play like this, he should try the Staunton Gambit; the additional moves 2 c4 and 2...e6 clearly favour Black.

3...fxe4

Naturally, Black should accept.

4 ♘c3 ♘f6

It is worth noting that 4...♗b4? is a mistake here since White can reply 5 ♕g4, winning his pawn back.

5 ♗g5

After 5 f3 ♗b4 6 ♕c2 ♘c6 7 ♗e3 e5 Black has the initiative as well as keeping his extra pawn.

5...♗b4

This shows the main difference between this gambit and the Staunton. Black rarely has the chance of playing ...♗b4 in the Staunton due to White replying c3.

6 f3 d5

6...exf3?! is playable but leads to the kind of position that White is looking for. After 7 ♘xf3 White has easy development and a ready-made attack due to Black's weakened kingside.

7 fxe4 dxe4 8 ♘e2 0-0

Black is slightly better.

C)

2 ♘f3 e6

Of course 2...♘f6 is an option, and would rule out White's next move. However, if you play a move-order with 1...e6 or 2...e6, then you will need to be ready to meet the following gambit:

3 e4!? *(D)*

This is one of White's trickier gambits, but with correct play Black should stand better at the end of the complications.

3...fxe4 4 ♘g5 ♘f6 5 f3

White's aim is to open up the f-file and the b1-h7 diagonal against the black king, after which he would have good attacking chances.

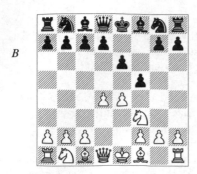

5...c5! *(D)*

This is an important move, by which Black strikes out at the white centre. Other moves give White the type of play he is seeking; e.g., 5...h6?! (this seriously weakens the black king) 6 ♘h3 exf3 7 ♕xf3, or 5...exf3?! 6 ♕xf3 when White will continue with ♗d3 and 0-0 with ready-made attacking chances.

6 fxe4 cxd4 7 ♗d3

Other moves don't help White: 7 e5? is met by 7...♕a5+, while 7 ♕xd4 ♘c6 8 ♕e3 b6 gives Black all the play, since his minor pieces are very active.

7...♘c6 8 0-0 ♗d6!

Another important move. Black must prevent White from playing e5 at all costs, and the bishop can come to rest happily on e5.

9 ♘d2

This is White's best attempt. Other moves make life easier for Black:

a) 9 c3 0-0 (9...♕c7? would give White dangerous play after 10 ♖xf6! and ♕h5+) 10 cxd4 ♘xd4 ∓ (if White does nothing here, Black should consolidate his position with ...♗e5!, ...b6 and ...♗b7, while ...♕c7 is also on the cards, forcing White to weaken his kingside) 11 e5?! (a desperate attempt which rebounds) 11...♗xe5 12 ♘xh7 ♘xh7 13 ♗xh7+ ♔xh7 14 ♕h5+ ♔g8 15 ♖xf8+ ♕xf8 16 ♕xe5 ♘c2 −+.

b) 9 ♘a3 gives Black a choice between two advantageous lines: 9...0-0 10 ♘c4, transposing to the main line, or 9...♘e5 10 ♘b5 ♗b8 11 ♔h1 0-0 12 ♘xd4 ♘fg4 13 ♘df3 ♘h6 (another option is 13...h6 14 ♘h3 b6).

9...0-0 10 ♘c4

Now:

a) 10...♗c7?! allows 11 e5! ♗xe5 12 ♘xe5 ♘xe5 13 ♘xh7 ♘xh7 14 ♗xh7+ ♔xh7 15 ♕h5+ ♔g8 16 ♖xf8+ ♕xf8 17 ♕xe5 =.

b) 10...♗e5! denies White compensation. 11 ♘f3 d6 leaves Black a pawn up with a solid position, while after 11 c3 dxc3! 12 ♘xe5 ♘xe5! Black is doing well.

D)

2 e4 *(D)*

This is the Staunton Gambit, which is popular with club players, but not so dangerous for Black if he knows what he is doing.

2...fxe4 3 ♘c3 ♘f6

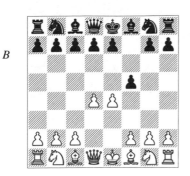

B

White has three ways of continuing, with Line D3 the most popular and reliable.

D1: 4 f3?!   89
D2: 4 g4   90
D3: 4 ♗g5   92

The first two are more of a real gambit than 4 ♗g5, since in Line D3 White normally regains his pawn.

D1)
4 f3?!
With correct play from Black, this is simply bad for White.

4...d5 *(D)*

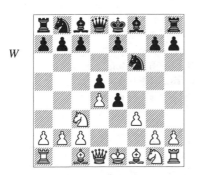

W

White wants Black to capture on f3, and it is always useful to deny your opponent his desires.

5 fxe4 dxe4

The e4-pawn has the useful function of denying White the f3- and d3-squares for his pieces.

6 ♗g5 ♘f5 7 ♗c4

This is the most dynamic move, taking the weakened a2-g8 diagonal, but it is not enough for equality. Other moves also pose little threat to Black; for example:

a) 7 ♘ge2?! (it's better to develop the light-squared bishop before moving this knight) 7...e6 8 ♘g3 ♗e7 9 ♕d2 h6 10 ♗e3 ♘bd7 11 ♗e2 ♘b6 12 0-0 ♕d7 13 ♘h5 ♖g8 14 ♘xf6+ ♗xf6 15 ♗h5+ g6 16 ♗e2 ♕g7 17 ♗xh6 ♗xd4+ 18 ♔h1 ♕h8 19 ♗f4 0-0-0 and Black was well on top in Gulko-M.Gurevich, USSR Ch (Riga) 1985.

b) 7 ♕e2?! was played as early as Ed.Lasker-Alekhine, Paris 1913, but it does not help White since on e2 the queen blocks in too many of White's pieces. Play continued 7...♘c6! 8 ♗xf6 exf6 9 0-0-0 ♗d6 (9...♕d7, followed by castling queenside, is even stronger) 10 ♘xe4 0-0 11 ♘xd6 cxd6 12 ♕f2 ♕a5 ∓. Black has potential to attack on the queenside, with the open c-file and more developed pieces.

7...♘c6 8 ♘ge2 e6! *(D)*

Black used to play 8...♕d7, but the text-move is simpler and better.

9 0-0 ♘a5

9...♗e7 also seems good for Black:

a) 10 ♗xf6 ♗xf6 11 d5 gets a bit messy, but Black is doing well after 11...♘a5 12 dxe6 ♕xd1 13 ♘xd1 ♘xc4 14 ♖xf5 ♘d6 ∓.

b) 10 ♕e1 ♘g4 11 ♗xe7 ♕xe7 ∓; e.g., 12 ♘g3 ♘xd4 13 ♘cxe4 0-0-0 14

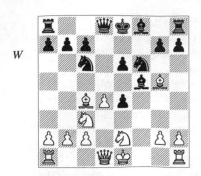

W

♕a5 ♔b8 15 ♖ae1 ♘xc2 and Black wins.

10 ♗xf6

10 ♗b5+ c6 is also good for Black. Once White's light-squared bishop is gone, he will find it very hard to attack the black king. 11 ♗a4 b5 12 ♗xf6 gxf6 (12...♕xf6 also looks good for Black; for example, 13 ♘xe4 ♕h4) 13 ♖xf5 (desperation, but otherwise Black will consolidate his extra pawn) 13...exf5 14 ♘g3 h5 (stopping ♕h5+) 15 ♘xf5 bxa4 16 ♘xe4 ♕c7 17 ♘xf6+ ♔d8 18 ♕e1 ♔c8 19 b4?! (19 ♘e8 ♕d7 20 ♕e5 ♔b7 ∓) 19...♕f7 20 bxa5 ♕xf6 21 ♕e8+ ♔c7 22 ♕xa8 ♗c5 −+.

10...♕xf6 11 ♗b3

11 ♘xe4? is a mistake owing to 11...♕h6 with a big attack: 12 ♘d2 ♗d6 ∓.

11...♗d6

Black has a large advantage. His bishops are too much of a force for White's knights. Liardet-Malaniuk, Geneva 1997 continued 12 ♘g3 ♘xb3 13 axb3 ♕h4 14 d5 0-0 (even better is 14...♗xg3! 15 hxg3 ♕xg3 16 dxe6 ♕e3+ 17 ♔h1 ♕h6+ 18 ♔g1 ♕xe6 ∓) 15 dxe6 ♗xe6 16 ♘cxe4 ♗e5 and Black won in a further 8 moves.

D2)

4 g4 *(D)*

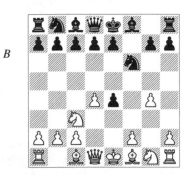

B

This is more of a 'real' gambit than 4 f3. This move also makes the white king weaker later on, which can play a significant role in Black's resources.

4...h6

It is now difficult for White to remove the good defensive knight from f6.

5 f3

Other moves are worse; for example, 5 g5 hxg5 6 ♗xg5 d5 7 h4?! (this seems a bit slow; 7 f3 is more to the point) 7...♘c6 8 f3 ♗f5 9 ♗h3 ♕d7 10 ♗xf5 ♕xf5 ∓ Dalkiran-Onishchuk, Iraklion ECC 1997.

5...d5

White has plenty of options here but none are too worrying for Black. Black's plan is normally to break out with ...e5 at the appropriate time. We discuss:

D21: 6 g5   91
D22: 6 h3   91

Other moves:

a) 6 fxe4 dxe4 (the alternative ideas 6...e5!? and 6...♗xg4!? are also interesting and look OK for Black) 7 h3 ♘c6 8 ♗e3 e5 is slightly better for Black.

b) 6 ♗f4 c5 7 ♘b5 ♘a6 8 dxc5 e5! 9 ♗xe5 ♗xc5 gives Black a slight advantage, Efimov – Santo-Roman, Nice 1994.

c) 6 ♗g2 c5 7 fxe4 cxd4 8 ♘xd5 ♘c6 9 ♘h3 e6 10 0-0? (this is a mistake but White's position is difficult anyway; for example, after 10 ♘xf6+ ♕xf6 ∓ White's king is looking rather exposed) 10...exd5 11 exd5 ♘xd5 12 ♕d3 ♘ce7 13 ♘f4 ♘xf4 14 ♗xf4 ♕b6 and Black is much better, Conquest-Malaniuk, Espergærde 1992.

D21)

6 g5 hxg5 7 ♗xg5 ♗f5 8 ♗g2

Other moves don't help either:

a) 8 ♕e2 ♘c6 9 0-0-0 ♕d7 10 ♗xf6 exf6 11 fxe4 dxe4 12 ♘xe4 0-0-0 13 d5 ♘b4 ∓.

b) White's best may be 8 ♕d2 but Black is fine if he just develops normally.

8...e3!

As so often occurs in gambits, returning the material secures an easy game.

9 ♘ge2 ♘c6 10 a3 e6 11 ♗xe3 ♗d6 12 ♗f4 ♗xf4 13 ♘xf4 ♕d6 14 ♕d2 ♖h4!

Forcing the white pieces into more passive roles.

15 ♘ce2 g5 16 ♘d3 ♘h7 17 f4 gxf4 18 ♘dxf4 0-0-0 19 0-0-0 ♘f6

Black has a nice position and a slight advantage. He has control over e4 and his pieces are on better squares than White's.

D22)

6 h3

After this move White's position looks like rather a mess, but nevertheless this is White's best option.

6...♘c6 7 fxe4

This capture is the best move in a difficult position. 7 ♗e3?! turns out badly: 7...e5 (given White's lack of development, Black strikes out in the centre) 8 dxe5 ♘xe5 9 f4 ♘f7 10 ♕d2 c6 ∓ Bronstein-M.Gurevich, Moscow 1987.

7...dxe4 8 ♗e3 *(D)*

Now:

a) Black can reach equality with the simple 8...e6 9 ♘ge2 ♗b4 10 ♕d2 ♗d7 11 a3 ♗xc3 12 ♘xc3 ♘e7 13 ♗g2 ♗c6 14 0-0-0 ♕d7 15 ♖he1 0-0-0 16 ♔g1 e3 17 ♖xe3 =.

b) 8...e5 9 dxe5! (9 ♘ge2 ♗b4 left Black a safe pawn up in the game Bouton-Malaniuk, Ubeda 1996) 9...♘xe5 10 ♕xd8+ ♔xd8 11 0-0-0+ ♗d7 12 ♗g2 ♗d6 13 ♘xe4 (13 ♘ge2 can be met by 13...♖e8) 13...♘xe4 14 ♗xe4 ♘c4 15 ♗d4 ♖e8 (not 15...♗f4+? 16 ♔b1 ♘d2+ 17 ♖xd2 ♗xd2 18 ♘f3 ±) 16 ♗f3 (16 ♗xb7? loses to 16...♗f4+

17 ♔b1 ♖b8 18 ♗f3 ♘a3+) 16...♖e7 =.

D3)
4 ♗g5 (D)

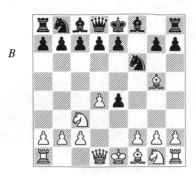

This is the main line. Black now has a couple of promising ideas.

4...♘c6

4...c6 is also reasonable: 5 f3 (5 ♗xf6 exf6 6 ♘xe4 d5 ∓ gives Black the advantage of the bishop-pair, with a solid position) 5...exf3 6 ♘xf3 d5 7 ♗d3 g6 (a common way of developing this bishop in the Staunton) and then:

a) 8 ♘e5 ♗g7 9 ♕e2 (9 h4 0-0 10 h5 ♘xh5 11 ♖xh5 ♗xe5 12 dxe5 ♕b6 is much better for Black) 9...0-0 10 0-0-0 ♘bd7 ∓.

b) 8 ♕d2 is a more dynamic way of playing; e.g., 8...♗g7 9 0-0-0 0-0 and here Black should push his a- and b-pawns, and meet h4 with ...♗g4, which is aimed against h5. The position is unclear but Black's chances can't be worse.

5 d5 ♘e5 6 ♕d4 ♘f7

On f7, the knight does a good job, defending and attacking.

7 ♗xf6

This is the most popular move but Black now has an unmatched dark-squared bishop, which will find a good home on the a1-h8 diagonal. Other moves:

a) 7 h4 is most simply met by 7...e5 8 dxe6 dxe6 9 ♕xd8+ ♘xd8 10 0-0-0 and now Black should play 10...♗d7 =, stopping ♘b5. Instead, 10...♘f7?, as in Cifuentes-Menvielle, Las Palmas 1993, is well met by 11 ♘b5! ♗d6 12 ♖xd6!; e.g., 12...cxd6 13 ♘c7+ ♔d8 14 ♘xa8 b6 15 ♖h3!! ♗b7 16 ♗xf6 gxf6 17 ♖a3 +−.

b) 7 ♘h3!? has not been tried very often but may be White's best attempt. Then:

b1) 7...e5?! (this may just suffice for equality, but it is hardly in the spirit of the opening) 8 dxe6 dxe6 9 ♕xd8+ ♘xd8 10 0-0-0 ♘f7? (10...♗d7 is equal) 11 ♗b5+? (11 ♘b5! ±) 11...c6 12 ♗c4 ♘d6 13 ♗b3 e5 14 ♖he1 h6 15 ♗h4 (Markov-Berkovich, Russian Cht (Podolsk) 1993) 15...♗xh3 16 gxh3 0-0-0 is about equal.

b2) 7...g6 and now:

b21) 8 ♗xf6 exf6 9 ♘xe4 ♗g7 10 d6 0-0 11 dxc7? (11 ♗c4 is a better attempt but it need not worry Black) 11...♕e7 12 ♕e3 ♖e8 13 f3 d5 0-1 was the embarrassing end in Beltramlini-Belmante, Pan American Ch 1996.

b22) 8 ♘xe4 ♗g7 9 ♗d2 c6 is fine for Black, P.Littlewood-Lund, British League (4NCL) 1996/7.

7...exf6 8 ♘xe4 f5

8...♗e7 is another viable option. The plan is to castle, and then play ...f5 and ...♗f6 at the right moment. After 9 0-0-0 0-0 White has two options:

a) 10 ♘g3 d6 and then:

a1) 11 ♗d3 ♘h6 (Black's plan as usual is to play a timely ...f5 and ...♗f6) 12 ♖e1 f5 13 ♘h5 ♖f7 14 ♔b1 c5 15 ♕e3 ♘g4 16 ♕e2 ♗d7 17 ♘f4 ♕a5 ∓ Brandenburg-Noetzel, Dieren 1991.

a2) 11 f4 c5 (this is nearly always a useful move as it gains space on the queenside, and if White replies dxc6 then Black has a strong centre) 12 ♕c3 ♘h6 13 ♗d3 f5 14 ♕d2 g6 15 h4 ♗f6 (it may be possible to capture on h4, but why bother, when Black can get on with his own attack?) 16 h5 ♘g4 17 ♘f3 ♗d7 18 hxg6 hxg6 (the f6-bishop is critical because it defends Black's kingside and puts pressure on White's queenside) 19 ♖h3 ♖e8 = Kravtsov-Vyzhmanavin, Russia Cup (Novgorod) 1997.

b) 10 f4 d6 (there is no rush for Black to play ...f5; the move ...d6 is useful as it stops White ever playing d6 himself, and Black can often play ...c5 gaining space on the queenside) 11 ♘f3 c5 12 ♕d2 ♗g4 (12...b5!? is interesting, when pressure against b2 follows shortly) 13 ♗e2 f5 14 ♘g3 ♕d7 15 h3 ♗xf3 16 ♗xf3 ∓. Black can now continue with either 16...♗h4 (Eis-S.Bücker, Bundesliga 1990/1) and doubling rooks on the e-file or 16...♗f6 followed by ...b5, ...b4, ...c4, etc. In both cases he holds a slight edge thanks to his more aggressive bishop.

9 ♘g3

After 9 ♘d2 ♕e7+ 10 ♗e2 g6 11 h4 ♗h6 12 h5 g5, rather than 13 ♔f1? ∓

Rogers-Van Mil, Tilburg 1993, White should settle for 13 0-0-0 =.

9...g6 10 0-0-0

After 10 h4?!, White's king will experience more difficulties than Black's: 10...♕e7+ 11 ♘1e2 ♗h6 12 h5 0-0 13 hxg6 hxg6 14 d6 ♕xd6 15 ♕xd6 cxd6 16 ♘c3 ♖e8+ 17 ♘ge2 ♖e5 ∓ Storland-Elsness, Norwegian Cht 2000.

10...♗h6+ 11 f4 0-0 12 ♘f3 ♗g7 13 ♕d2 (D)

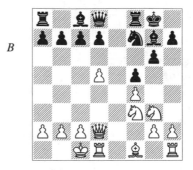

13...b5

13...c5 is another option; for example, 14 d6 b5 15 h4 h5 16 ♘g5 ♖b8 17 ♗e2 ♕f6 18 c3 ♖b6 (18...♔h8 followed by 19...b4 is another good idea) 19 ♘xf7 ♖xf7 20 ♗f3 ♗b7 21 ♗xb7 ♖xb7 22 ♕d5 ♖b6 23 ♖he1 ♗f8 24 ♖e8 ♔g7 with an equal position, Kerr-R.Meulders, London Aaronson Masters 1979.

14 c3 ♖b8 15 h4 h5 16 ♖e1 ♖b6 17 ♗d3 ♗b7 18 ♗c2

Black has a small edge. Naumann-Kindermann, Austrian Cht 2001/2 now continued 18...♖d6 (another option is the immediate 18...a5) 19 ♗b3 a5.

9 Early Deviations for White after 1 d4 f5

1 d4 f5

White and Black both have a number of ways of playing against the Dutch and with the Dutch. This is one of the reasons why Black should never get bored with this opening! In this chapter we shall consider early deviations by White.

Apart from the gambits we looked at in the previous chapter, White has three other sensible options on move two:

A: 2 ♘f3   94
B: 2 ♗g5   98
C: 2 ♘c3   101

In Line A we only discuss ideas for White that have not been dealt with elsewhere.

A)

2 ♘f3 e6

Now we consider three moves for White:

A1: 3 ♗g5   94
A2: 3 h3   95
A3: 3 d5!?   97

A1)

3 ♗g5 *(D)*

This continuation should not rattle Black.

3...♗e7

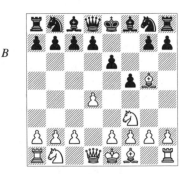

B

Why not exchange an undeveloped piece for a developed one? Black should normally avoid a Stonewall set-up after the exchange of dark-squared bishops, unless he can force ...e5, as his e5-square will be weak. However, a Classical set-up with a pawn on d6 will suit his purposes. White can now choose between two plans:

A11: 4 h4?!   94
A12: 4 ♗xe7   95

A11)

4 h4?!

This aggressive move will become a weakness later on in the game, and White will always have to think twice about castling kingside.

4...♘f6 *(D)*

This is simple and good; the move 4 h4?! looks useless now.

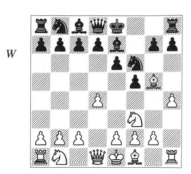

5 ⟁bd2

If 5 c3 then 5...b6 =. S.Ledger-S.Williams, British Ch (Nottingham) 1997 continued 6 ⟁bd2 ⟁b7 7 e3 0-0 8 ⟁d3 d5 (stopping any plans White might have had of playing e4) 9 ⟁e5 ⟁bd7 10 ⟁xd7 ⟕xd7 11 f4?! ⟁g4 and now Black was slightly better.

5...⟁e4

Another option is 5...d5, reaching a solid Stonewall structure where the h4-pawn will become a target; another interesting idea is 5...⟁c6!?.

6 e3 0-0 7 ⟁f4 d5 8 c4 ⟁d7 9 a3 ⟁df6 10 g3 b6

= Korchnoi-Wach, Ptuj Z 1995.

A12)

4 ⟁xe7 ⟕xe7 5 ⟁bd2

Or 5 ⟁c3 ⟁f6, and then:

a) 6 ⟕d3 (trying to force through e4) 6...⟁c6! 7 a3 d5 8 h3 e5! (forcing play) 9 dxe5 ⟁xe5 10 ⟁xe5 ⟕xe5 11 0-0-0 c6 ∓ I.Ivanov-Bronstein, Kishinev 1975.

b) 6 e3 d6 7 ⟁c4 c6 8 a4 a5 9 0-0 0-0 10 ⟖a3 ⟔h8 11 ⟁d2 e5 12 dxe5 dxe5 13 e4 f4! ∓ Haygarth-Bellin, British Ch (Ayr) 1978. A model example of how to play the opening by Black.

5...⟁f6 *(D)*

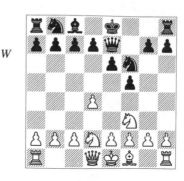

6 g3

White's set-up reveals a lack of Dutch understanding. Other moves:

a) 6 c3 c5 (other good options for Black are 6...b6 and 6...d6 with the standard plan of controlling the centre and playing ...e5 at the right moment) 7 ⟕c2 cxd4 8 cxd4 ⟁c6 = 9 a3 b6 10 e4 fxe4 11 ⟁xe4 ⟁xe4 12 ⟕xe4 ⟁b7, Schandorff-L.B.Hansen, Danish Ch (Lyngby) 1991.

b) 6 e3 d6 (again ...e5 is the right idea) 7 ⟁d3 e5 =.

6...0-0 7 ⟁g2 d6!

As usual, ...e5 is part of Black's plan.

8 c3 ⟁c6 9 ⟕c2 e5 10 dxe5 dxe5 11 e4 f4!

Another thematic move, ensuring Black an easy game and a slight advantage, Ubezlo-Naumkin, Saint Vincent 1998.

A2)

3 h3

With this move White plans either an early g4 push in the hope of opening some lines against Black's king, or the more sedate plan of making a re-treat-square for the queen's bishop after it moves to f4.

3...♘f6 4 ♗f4 b6

Black can safely place his bishop on the a8-h1 diagonal here since White has not fianchettoed his king's bishop. The best place for Black's bishop, if he can get it there, is the long diagonal. White now has two ways of playing, one of which is a lot more sedate than the other:

A21: 5 g4!?   96
A22: 5 e3   96

A21)

5 g4!? *(D)*

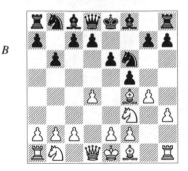

Playing like this is very risky since Black has control over the important central squares d5 and e4.

5...♗b7 6 ♘bd2 c5

It makes sense to strike out against the white centre.

7 e3 ♘c6

There is a complicated battle ahead, where Black's chances are no worse. Note that the greedy 7...fxg4? is not what Black should be doing. Taking this pawn gives White the kind of play

any Dutch player will cringe to see: 8 hxg4 ♘xg4 9 ♗d3 ♘h6? 10 ♖xh6 gxh6 11 ♘g5 ♕f6 12 ♕h5+ ♔e7 13 ♗d6+ ♔d8 14 ♘f7+ ♔c8 15 ♗e5 1-0 was the embarrassing end to Mozny-Relange, Clichy 1991.

A22)

5 e3 ♗b7 6 ♗d3 ♗e7 7 ♘bd2

White's plan as usual is to play e4. If he can achieve this, his extra space in the centre will give him the advantage. However, with Black's bishop on b7 and the possibility of him placing a piece on e4, White is going to find it very hard to achieve the e4 push.

7...0-0 8 c3 *(D)*

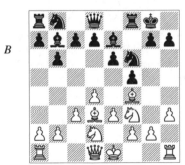

8...♗e4!?

This is a relatively recent idea. 8...♘e4 was previously thought to be the best but White may be able to get a slight advantage against this. Another decent plan for Black is 8...c5 9 ♕c2 ♘c6 10 dxc5 (10 e4? leaves the f4-bishop *en prise* to the f8-rook after an exchange on e4) 10...♗xc5 11 ♗h2 ♖c8 12 a3 (not 12 e4? ♘b4 13 cxb4 ♗xf2+ 14 ♔xf2 ♖xc2 15 ♗xc2 fxe4 ∓) 12...d5 = and Black is doing fine,

Chibukhchian-N.Pert, Erevan jr Wch 1999.

9 ♗xe4

It is nearly always beneficial for White to exchange this bishop in the Dutch. White's other options aren't inspiring either. After 9 ♕e2 d5 or 9 ♕c2 d5 Black can follow up with ...c5 and ...♘c6 with a perfectly satisfactory Stonewall, and can reckon on equality. If White tries to avoid the exchange of bishops with 9 ♗e2 then Black can reply 9...♗b7, when White will find it hard to play e4 without his bishop on d3. Black's plan is ...d6, ...♘e4, ...♘bd7 and ...♘df6.

9...♘xe4 10 ♘xe4 fxe4 11 ♘d2 d5

Black has equalized.

12 0-0

After 12 c4 ♘d7 Black intends to continue with 13...c5.

12...c5 13 f3

White could also try 13 dxc5 but Black is fine after 13...bxc5 14 c4?! ♕b6! 15 ♕c2 (15 ♖b1 ♘c6 16 a3 ♖ad8 ∓ or 15 cxd5 exd5 16 ♘xe4? dxe4 17 ♕d5+ ♔h8 18 ♕xa8 ♘c6 −+) 15...♘c6 16 a3 ♘d4 ∓.

13...exf3 14 ♕xf3 ♘c6 15 ♕g3 ♕d7 16 ♘f3 ♖f5 (D)

17 dxc5?!

Realizing he hasn't achieved any advantage from the opening, White overpresses; after this Black is better. White should play 17 ♘e5 ♘xe5 18 ♗xe5 ♖g5 19 ♕e1 ♖f5 = when the game should end in a draw.

17...bxc5 18 e4 dxe4 19 ♘d2 ♖af8 20 ♘xe4 ♕d5 21 ♕e3 ♘d4!

∓ Diachkov-Ulybin, Russian Clubs Cup (Maikop) 1998.

A3)

3 d5!? (D)

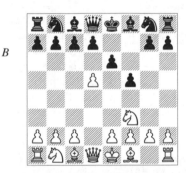

This interesting attempt to confuse matters has become popular recently. However, Black has a couple of ways of reaching dynamic equality.

3...♗d6

This is the simplest, but Black's other options are also OK:

a) 3...exd5 4 ♕xd5 can get very messy, but is an interesting option. 4...♕f6!? is an untried idea here, and looks OK for Black.

b) 3...♗b4+ has the idea of provoking White to put a pawn on c3 so his knight can't move there. However, it does allow White's queen another route out, via the d1-a4 diagonal. 4 c3 (other moves don't promise White anything; after 4 ♗d2?! ♕e7, given the chance Black will capture on d2 and play ...e5 with the advantage) 4...♗d6 5 dxe6 dxe6 and then:

b1) 6 ♘bd2 (intending the annoying ♘c4) gives Black no problems if he replies 6...♗c5! followed ideally by ...♘f6, ...0-0 and ...e5.

b2) 6 e4 fxe4 7 ♘g5 ♘f6 and now:

b21) 8 ♗b5+?! (now White wants Black to play ...c6!) 8...♗d7 9 ♕e2 ♗xb5 10 ♕xb5+ ♘bd7 11 ♗e3 (11 ♘xe6? ♕e7 12 ♘d4 0-0-0 ∓) 11...h6 12 ♘xe6 ♕e7 13 ♕b3 ♘e5 and Black is slightly better, Rowson-S.Williams, British League (4NCL) 1999/00.

b22) 8 ♘xe4 (this is best) 8...♘xe4 9 ♕a4+ ♘c6 10 ♕xe4 (the position is about equal; Black has the f-file and more developed pieces but his e6-pawn could become a weakness) 10...♗d7 11 ♘d2 ♕f6 12 ♕f3 ♕e5+ (another option is 12...0-0-0 =) 13 ♗e2 ♖f8 14 ♕h5+ ♕xh5 15 ♗xh5+ ♔e7 = Lalić-Narciso Dublan, Andorra la Vella 1999.

4 e4

Other moves:

a) 4 dxe6 dxe6 5 e4 fxe4 6 ♘g5 ♗b4+! (the safest way to reach equality) 7 c3 ♕xd1+ 8 ♔xd1 ♗e7 9 ♘xe4 ♘f6 10 ♘xf6+ (10 ♗d3 is probably better but the position is still about equal) 10...gxf6 11 ♗c4 e5 12 ♗h6 ♗f8 13 ♗e3 ♗f5 is equal, Zsu.Polgar-Schmitzer, Wiesbaden 1994.

b) 4 ♘c3 ♘f6 and then:

b1) 5 g3?! (this move looks a bit strange, since the bishop belongs on

c4) 5...0-0 6 ♗g2 c6 7 dxe6 dxe6 8 0-0 e5 9 e4 ♘a6 10 ♕e2 ♘c5 11 exf5 ♗xf5 (Black's isolated pawn is not that important since his pieces are all developed and active) 12 ♘g5 ♔h8 13 ♘ce4 ♘cxe4 14 ♘xe4 ♗xe4 15 ♗xe4 ♗c5 16 ♗g5 ♕b6 17 ♗xf6 ♖xf6 ∓ McDonald-S.Williams, British League (4NCL) 1999/00. Black's pressure on f2 gives him an easy game.

b2) 5 ♘b5 0-0 6 ♘xd6 cxd6 7 dxe6 dxe6 8 g3 b6 9 ♗g2 ♗b7 10 0-0 ♕e7 11 b3 ♘bd7 12 ♗b2 and Black is at least equal due to his central pawn majority, Barsov-Kerkmeester, Wijk aan Zee 1998.

4...fxe4 5 ♘g5 exd5!? 6 ♕xd5 ♕e7 7 ♗c4 ♘f6 8 ♕f7+ ♕xf7 9 ♘xf7 ♗b4+ *(D)*

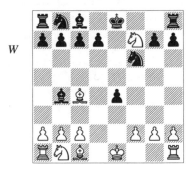

W

10 c3 ♖f8 11 cxb4 d5 12 ♘e5 dxc4 ∓ Adianto-Teske, Koszalin 1998.

B)

2 ♗g5!? *(D)*

This is an interesting move in the spirit of the Trompowsky. It stops normal development by Black with ...e6 and aims to double Black's pawns if he plays ...♘f6.

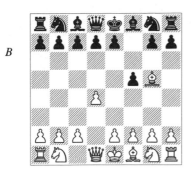

B

2...h6

This is the most interesting reply. Black puts the question to White's bishop.

3 ♗h4

White has another option here in 3 ♗f4. White is trying to prove that ...h6 has seriously weakened Black's kingside, and there are ideas of a quick e4. 3...♘f6 4 ♘c3 and now a routine response can easily land Black in trouble:

a) 4...d5 transposes to Line C41, where White retains a slight advantage.

b) 4...d6?! intends ...g5 and ...♗g7, but 5 e4! *(D)* gives White a big initiative since it exploits Black's complex of weak light squares:

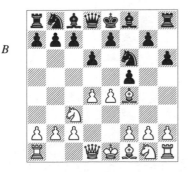

B

b1) 5...g5 6 e5 ♘g4 7 h3 dxe5 8 hxg4 exf4 9 gxf5 ♗xf5 10 ♕h5+ ♔d7 and Black's king is in mortal danger, Peshina-Avshalumov, USSR 1988.

b2) 5...fxe4 6 ♘xe4 ♘xe4 7 ♕h5+ ♔d7 8 ♕f5+ e6 9 ♕xe4 ♕f6 10 0-0-0 ♗e7 11 ♘f3 gives White a slight advantage, Ward-Sø.B.Hansen, Isle of Man 1994.

c) 4...e6! *(D)* has only been played twice but it looks perfectly satisfactory for Black.

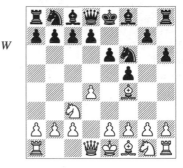

W

White has tried two continuations here:

c1) 5 e3 ♗b4 = (Black can also play ...b6 and ...♗b7 with an equal position) 6 a3 ♗xc3+ 7 bxc3 0-0 8 c4 d6 9 h3 ♘bd7 10 ♘f3 (Anguix-Mas Garc, Spanish Cht 1993) and now Black should play 10...♕e7 with the idea of moving forward in the centre with 11...e5, when he can be happy with his position.

c2) 5 e4 (this attempt to kill Black off should not work) 5...fxe4 6 f3 ♗b4 (6...d5, holding on to the pawn, is also OK) 7 fxe4 0-0 8 ♕d3 d5 9 exd5 exd5 10 0-0-0 = Romero-Gomez Esteban, Leon 1994.

3...g5 (D)

The reason why Black plays ...g5 is so that he can develop his king's knight without being saddled with doubled pawns. The extra space gained on the kingside can turn out to be more of a weakness than a strength after White hits out at it with h4, but at the moment it seems that Black can maintain equality.

White now has two principal ways of playing:

B1: 4 e3   100
B2: 4 e4   100

The latter is the more dangerous.

4 ♗g3 shouldn't hold any worries for Black, and will probably transpose to Line B1. Black should reply 4...♗g7 (this is better than 4...♘f6 since the g7-bishop, unobstructed by a knight on f6, supports the ...e5 break), when 5 e3 transposes to Line B1.

B1)

4 e3 ♗g7 5 ♗g3

5 ♕h5+ does not help White since the queen will lose time when it is chased away by the black knight, and the black king is safe behind its row of pawns: 5...♔f8 6 ♗g3 ♘f6 7 ♕f3 d6 8 ♗d3 ♘c6! 9 ♘c3 (9 ♗xf5? g4 10 ♕f4 e5 −+) 9...e5 10 dxe5 dxe5 11 0-0-0 ♕e7 (White can't avoid losing a piece) 12 ♗c4 f4 ∓ Lys-A.Andersen, Olomouc 2001.

5...d6

Again ...e5 is on the cards.

6 h4

6 ♗d3 ♘c6 7 c3 e5 8 h4 g4 9 h5 ♕e7 10 ♕c2 ♕f7 = M.Gretarsson-Danner, Oberwart 1996.

6...g4 7 ♘e2 e5

Black has equalized.

B2)

4 e4

This is White's sharpest reply.

4...♘f6

This is Black's only good move, and creates a strange position.

4...♗g7? has been played very often but it has a major failing: 5 ♗g3 f4 6 ♗xf4! gxf4 7 ♕h5+ ♔f8 8 ♕f5+ ♔e8 and now White can force a draw with ♕h5+ and ♕f5+, but he can certainly play for a win with 9 ♗e2 ♘f6 10 e5 e6 11 ♕xf4 ±.

5 e5 e6 6 exf6 ♕xf6 7 ♗g3 f4 (D)

8 ♗d3!

This is White's best attempt at getting anything from the opening. Other moves don't promise White any advantage:

a) The normal developing move 8 ♘c3 runs into 8...♗b4, which is annoying for White.

b) 8 ♘f3 and then:

b1) 8...♘c6 is a sound option. 9 c3 (again 9 ♘c3 runs into the pin 9...♗b4) 9...d6 10 ♘bd2 ♗d7 11 ♘e4 ♕e7 12 ♗xf4 (12 ♗d3 0-0-0 13 ♕e2 ♗g7) 12...gxf4 13 ♕d2 ♕f7 = and Black is OK: his king is safe and he has the bishop-pair and the open g-file.

b2) 8...fxg3 9 hxg3 ♘c6 10 c3 d5 11 ♗b5 ♗d6 12 ♗xc6+ bxc6 13 ♕e2 a5! = Claesen-Meulders, Belgian Cht 2001. The bishop wants to go to a6.

8...♘c6 9 ♕h5+ ♔d8

The king is safe hiding behind the central pawns.

10 c3 d5

There is another option in the untried 10...e5 11 d5 ♘e7 12 ♘d2, with an unclear position.

11 ♘f3 ♗d7 12 0-0 ♗d6 13 ♘bd2 ♔e7 14 ♖ae1 ♖ag8

Now:

a) 15 ♘e5?! ♘xe5 16 dxe5 ♗xe5 17 ♘b3 ♗d6 gives Black a slight advantage, Moiseenko-Jakubiec, Polanica Zdroj 1999.

b) 15 ♘b3! is the best move, when play might continue 15...♗e8 16 ♕g4 ♔f7 17 ♘c5 ♗xc5 18 dxc5, with an unclear position where White might hold a small advantage. 18...♗d7 looks like the best move, when White has to keep an eye on his queen.

C)

2 ♘c3 *(D)*

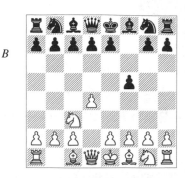

B

In my opinion, this simple developing move is White's most dangerous non-standard response to the Dutch. White intends to play a quick e4, followed by an attack against the black king with developing moves. Leaving the pawn on c2 gives White more time to expose the black king. This is similar in spirit to 2 ♗g5, as White very often follows up with ♗g5 in order to double Black's pawns or to try to force e4. Black has to play accurately to achieve a satisfactory position.

2...d5

I do not like 2...♘f6 since after 3 ♗g5! White will either double Black's pawns or force the e4 break, in both cases holding on to a nice advantage without too much effort.

With the text-move, Black adopts a Stonewall structure. This makes sense here since it will take White quite a while to attack d5 with his c-pawn, given the knight's position on c3. Thus White generally seeks to control the dark squares (in particular f4 and e5) with his pieces.

Now White has a number of replies.

C1: 3 e4?!　　102
C2: 3 ♘f3　　103
C3: 3 ♗f4　　103
C4: 3 ♗g5!　　104

As the markings indicate, the fourth option is the most troublesome for Black.

You might occasionally come across 3 g4?!, but if White wishes to play a gambit, he has a lot of better options than this. 3...♘f6 (3...fxg4 will probably transpose to other gambit lines where Black is doing fine) 4 g5 ♘e4 5 ♘xe4 fxe4 6 f3 ♗f5 ∓ Spielmann-Mieses, Berlin 1920.

C1)

3 e4?!

This attempt by White to trick Black into reaching a bad Staunton Gambit demands an accurate response.

3...dxe4! (D)

Black is doing fine due to the pressure against White's d-pawn. Instead, 3...fxe4? is simply a mistake, since it reaches an inferior variation of the Staunton Gambit: 4 ♕h5+ g6 5 ♕xd5 ±.

It is worth noting that 3...e5 is also a playable move, reaching a very peculiar position.

4 ♗f4

Stopping ...e5 but losing time.

Instead, 4 f3 allows the thematic 4...e5!, exploiting the half-open d-file. 5 dxe5 ♕xd1+ 6 ♔xd1 ♘c6! (6...♗e6 is also OK, but Black is looking for more) 7 ♘d5 ♔d8 8 ♗g5+ ♘ge7 9 f4 h6 10 ♘xe7 ♘xe7! 11 ♗xe7+ ♔xe7 12

c3 ♗e6 13 ♔c2 ♔f7 14 ♘e2 ♗c5 15 ♖d1 ♗e3 16 g3 g5 ∓ V.Milov-Kramnik, USSR 1990. Black's bishop-pair and extra space assure him a pleasant game.

4...♘f6 5 f3 e6 6 fxe4

Not 6 ♗c4? due to 6...♘d5, when Black is much better.

6...fxe4 7 ♗c4

7 ♕d2 followed by 0-0-0 is another try, but Black should be fine if he plays normal developing moves.

7...♘c6 8 ♘ge2 ♘a5! (D)

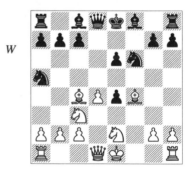

Simplifying matters.

9 ♗b3

9 ♗b5+ c6 10 ♗a4 b5 11 ♗b3 ∓ is similar, but Black has the extra option of playing ...b4.

9...♞xb3 10 axb3 ♝d7 11 ♞g3 ♝c6 12 0-0

Now Black played 12...♝e7?! in the game Benjamin-Malaniuk, Moscow 1987 which is a slight mistake, but 12...♝d6! ∓, again simplifying matters, would have left him with a nice advantage.

C2)

3 ♞f3 ♞f6 4 g3?!

This set-up doesn't fit in with an early ♞c3; the light-squared bishop should go to d3. On g2 it will be staring against the rock of a pawn on d5. If White could quickly play c4, he might create some meaningful pressure on d5, but this is not the case here, so Black is doing well. It seems that the only way Black has any problems in this line is when White develops his c1-bishop at an early stage.

4...e6 5 ♝g2 c5! *(D)*

Making use of White's lame set-up.

6 0-0 cxd4 7 ♞b5 ♝d7 8 ♞bxd4 ♞c6 9 c4

A bit late.

9...dxc4 10 ♕c2 ♖c8 11 ♞xc6 ♝xc6 12 ♕xc4

Siegel-Vallejo Pons, Havana Capablanca mem 1998. Now Black should play 12...♕d5 13 ♕xd5 ♝xd5 with a slight advantage.

C3)

3 ♝f4

This diagonal is the most natural place for the white bishop, as it controls the all-important e5-square and puts pressure on c7. However, 3 ♝g5 is more annoying for Black, as it puts him off playing the natural 3...♞f6 due to White doubling his pawns with 4 ♝xf6.

3...c6

One of White's ideas is to play ♞b5 followed by c4, gaining space on the queenside, so Black stops this plan.

4 e3 ♞f6 5 ♝d3 e6 6 ♞f3 ♝e7 7 0-0

Black can be happy with the outcome of the opening: he has an advantageous Stonewall set-up, since White hasn't expanded on the queenside with c4.

7...0-0 8 ♞e2 ♞bd7 9 h3

9 c4 ♞e4 (another option for Black is 9...♞h5!?, with the idea of playing ...g5 and capturing White's important dark-squared bishop) 10 ♞e5 ♝f6 (Black plans to simplify matters) 11 ♕c2 g5 12 ♞xd7 ♝xd7 13 ♝e5 g4 14 ♔h1?! ♝xe5 15 dxe5 ♕c7 16 cxd5 exd5 17 f4 gxf3 18 gxf3 ♕xe5! and Black is doing well, Izeta-Ochoa, Gran Canaria 1993.

9...♞e4 10 c4 ♝f6 11 b4 ♕e7 12 ♕b3 g5 13 ♝h2 h5 *(D)*

Black gains sufficient play on the kingside.

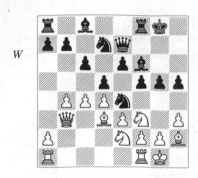

14 ♗xe4 fxe4 15 ♘d2 ♗g7 16 f3 exf3 17 ♘xf3 g4

The position is equal, I.Sokolov-P.Nikolić, Sremić Krsko ECC 1998.

C4)
    3 ♗g5! (D)

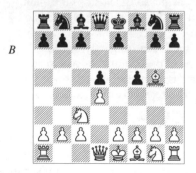

This is the most annoying move for Black to deal with, since the natural 3...♘f6 lets White double Black's pawns with 4 ♗xf6. There are a number of ways that Black can reply, but most of them give White a small safe advantage. However, I believe there is an option for Black that is risky but doesn't guarantee White an advantage, namely 3...c6!. Still, I shall present two possible options, to accommodate

a broader range of stylistic preferences:

After the former I believe White can keep a small advantage. 3...c6! is more testing; play becomes sharp and Black must defend for a while, but it does not seem that White can achieve an advantage.

C41)
    3...h6

Kicking the bishop away is natural, but it seems that White can now retain a slight edge. The difference between this and Line C3 (3 ♗f4) is that Black has weakened himself on the e8-h5 diagonal and especially the g6-square. White can aim to land a knight on g6 in some situations.

    4 ♗f4 ♘f6 (D)

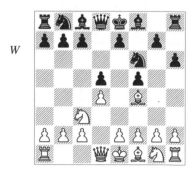

5 e3
Other moves:

a) 5 e4?! is both over-optimistic and misguided as White can achieve a slight advantage playing normal moves – there is no need to sacrifice any material. 5...fxe4 6 f3 ♗f5 (this position resembles the 1 d4 f5 2 ♘c3 d5 3 e4 line, where Black is doing well; it differs from the Staunton Gambit, in that White can no longer regain his pawn with ♗g5 and ♗xf6) 7 fxe4 dxe4 8 ♗c4 e6 9 ♘ge2 ♘c6 (Black's plan is to play ...♘a5, exchanging off White's powerful c4-bishop) 10 a3 ♗d6 (exchanging White's attacking pieces; not 10...♘a5?! owing to 11 ♗a2) 11 0-0 ♗xf4 12 ♖xf4 ♕e7 13 ♔h1 0-0-0 14 ♕g1 ♔b8 15 ♖ff1 h5 ∓ Conquest-Kindermann, Baden-Baden 1993. Black has all the play.

b) 5 ♘f3 (D) will normally transpose to the main line. Black has two ways of playing here: he can leave the pawn on c7 and play ...♗d6 (which seems best) or else play ...c6 and go for a Stonewall-type set-up:

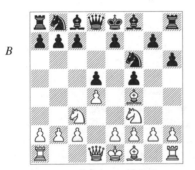

b1) 5...c6 leads to similar positions to those reached in Line C3 (3 ♗f4). The only difference is that Black has a pawn on h6 instead of h7, which is advantageous to White as he can try to land a knight on g6 at some point. Black can try covering the holes around his kingside with ...♗e6 and ...♗f7 at the right moment but this also gives

him trouble. 6 e3 g5!? (this looks like Black's best try) 7 ♗g3 ♗g7 8 ♗d3 0-0 9 h4 g4 10 ♘e5 ♕e8 11 ♘e2 ♘h5 12 ♗h2 ♘d7 13 ♕d2 = Upero-Latvio, Lahtu 2000. The ...g5!? idea looks a bit suspect as Black has a big hole on e5 which he will never be able to cover, and his kingside also looks a bit shaky. Therefore, I'm sure White can improve somewhere and retain a small advantage.

b2) After 5...e6 6 e3 ♗d6 White has to play accurately to achieve any kind of advantage:

b21) 7 ♘e5?! (Black is fine after this) 7...0-0 8 ♗d3 (8 ♘b5 ♘c6 9 ♘g6 ♖e8 and Black can achieve counterplay with the break ...e5; he also has ideas of pushing back the g6-knight with ...♔h7, when it will be short of squares) 8...♘bd7 = 9 ♘g6 ♖e8 10 ♗xd6 cxd6 11 0-0 ♘b8 12 f3 ♔f7 13 ♘f4 g5 14 ♘fe2 e5 15 e4 dxe4 16 fxe4 f4 17 dxe5 dxe5 18 ♗c4+ ♗e6 19 ♗xe6+ ♔xe6 20 ♕e1 ♘c6 ∓ Nikitin-Nureev, Russian Cht 2001.

b22) 7 ♘b5! hasn't been tried yet but represents the logical continuation of White's play. He plans to capture on d6 with his knight and play c4, undermining Black's centre. This would assure him a small lasting advantage. Black should reply 7...♘c6, when play might continue 8 c4 g5 – White has the advantage but Black is reasonably solid.

5...e6

Black can also aim for a Stonewall set-up with 5...c6, which has the advantage of stopping any ideas involving ♘b5 and c4. Then:

a) 6 ♗e2?! g6!? (White will find it hard to play c4 due to the bishop being on e2, as White's normal plan involves ♘ce2 and c4) 7 ♘f3 ♗e6!? (from f7 the bishop does a good job of defending Black's kingside) 8 ♘e5 ♖g8 9 h4 ♘bd7 10 ♘d3 ♗f7 11 ♕d2 e6 12 f3 g5 13 hxg5 hxg5 14 ♗h2 ♗g7 15 0-0-0 ♕e7 = Partanen-Valkesalmi, Finnish Ch (Helsinki) 1988.

b) 6 ♘f3 transposes to note 'b1' to White's 5th move, which is better for White.

6 ♗d3

6 ♘b5 is an interesting alternative. 6...♗d6 7 ♘xd6+ cxd6 (Black plans on playing a quick ...e5) and now:

a) 8 h3?! ♘c6 9 ♘f3 0-0 10 c3 ♕e7 = 11 ♗b5 ♗d7 12 ♗h2 ♗e8 13 ♕a4 ♘e4 14 ♕a3 g5 15 ♗d3 f4 16 ♗xe4 dxe4 17 ♘d2 ♗g6 ∓ Degerman-E.Berg, Swedish Ch (Ronneby) 1998.

b) 8 ♘f3! is better. White's priority is to develop quickly and try to achieve the c4 break before Black plays ...e5. White then holds a small advantage.

6...♗d6

With correct play it appears that White gets a nice advantage against this natural move.

7 ♘f3 0-0 (D)

Other moves:

a) After 7...♘c6 White should continue with the standard plan of advancing c4, which will give him an advantage: 8 ♘e2 ♘b4?! 9 c4 ♘xd3+ 10 ♕xd3 c6 ± and Black has ended up with a bad bishop against a good knight. White will eventually land his knight on e5.

b) 7...c5 allows the strong plan of 8 ♗b5+!, disrupting Black's position: 8...♘c6 9 ♘e5 ±.

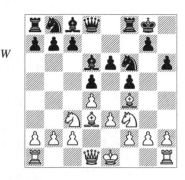

W

8 ♘e2!

Again White is making up for not playing c4 earlier. The knight will move to f4 at some point, homing in on the weakness on g6. Other moves do not trouble Black:

a) 8 ♘e5?! is premature and allows Black to simplify with 8...♘c6 9 ♘xc6 bxc6 10 ♘a4 ♕e7 11 0-0 e5 = Soffer-Rechlis, Berne 1990.

b) 8 ♘b5 is normally a sensible plan – the idea as before is to play ♘xd6 and c4, but here Black can counter with the ...e5 break: 8...♘c6 (again Black should aim for ...e5 with ...♕e7, and also possibly ...g5) and now play might continue 9 ♘xd6 cxd6 10 0-0 (the immediate 10 c4 gives Black the option of 10...♕a5+) and Black can choose between 10...♖e8, 10...♕e7 and 10...♘h5, with approximate equality in all cases.

8...c5

Black must try to gain space before White plays c4 with a safe advantage. Now:

a) 9 c3?! was met by the inferior 9...b6? in the game Vaïsser-Szabolcsi, France 1993. Black should instead play 9...♘c6!, since it is important to try to exchange as many pieces as possible on the e5-square. White may be able to keep a small advantage but Black has more space and possibilities of expanding in the centre. Play might continue 10 ♗xd6 ♕xd6 11 ♘f4 (trying to highlight the weakness on g6) 11...♔h7, when Black's plans include ...e5, ...♘e4 and even ...g5. For example:

a1) 12 0-0 g5 13 ♘e2 e5! and Black has no worries.

a2) After 12 dxc5 ♕xc5 13 ♘d4 ♕d6 = any attempt to blow Black away will backfire; for example, 14 g4? ♘xd4 15 cxd4 ♕b4+ – greed is sometimes a good idea.

a3) 12 ♗c2 (with the idea of playing 13 ♘d3 with a hold on the e5-square) 12...e5! and Black can even claim to be slightly better.

b) 9 c4! gives White a small advantage, because the f5-pawn is a long-term weakness. Play might continue 9...cxd4 10 exd4 ♗b4+ 11 ♘c3, when White is significantly better.

C42)

3...c6! (D)

Black is looking to play 4...♕b6 followed by ...♘d7 and ...♘gf6, avoiding doubled f-pawns, and bearing down on White's queenside. This is normally followed up by Black fianchettoing his dark-squared bishop, and hopefully advancing ...e5 at some point.

White's most testing here is...

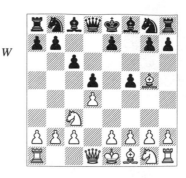

W

4 e4!

This aggressive gambit gives White an initiative in return for a pawn. The positions are similar to those from the Staunton Gambit, but Black has spent time playing ...c6. Other moves need not worry Black.

After 4 e3?! ♕b6 White has tried:

a) 5 ♖b1 ♘d7 (Black rightly continues with normal development) 6 ♗d3 g6 7 h4 ♗g7 8 h5 h6 9 ♗f4 g5 10 ♗h2 e5! 11 ♗xf5 exd4 12 exd4 ♘e7 and now:

a1) 13 ♗xd7+ ♗xd7 is absolutely fine for Black whether White opts for 14 ♘ge2, 14 ♘ce2 ♗g4, 14 ♘f3 ♗g4 15 ♗e5 ♗xe5 16 dxe5 ♖f8 or 14 ♗e5 ♗xe5 15 dxe5 ♕c7.

a2) 13 ♕e2 was played in I.Sokolov-P.Nikolić, Dutch Ch (Rotterdam) 1998) and now 13...♗xd4! gives Black a sizeable advantage; e.g., 14 ♘d1 (14 ♗xd7+ doesn't help White: 14...♗xd7 15 ♗e5 ♗xe5 16 ♕xe5 0-0-0 ∓) 14...♔d8! 15 ♗xd7 ♗xd7 ∓.

b) 5 a3 has the intention of meeting ...♕xb2 with ♘a4, winning the black queen. Black should continue with 5...♘d7 6 ♗d3 g6 7 ♘f3 (after 7 h4 ♗g7! 8 h5 h6 9 ♗f4 g5 10 ♗g3 e6 =

Black is doing well) 7...♗g7 8 ♗f4 ♘h6 9 b4 ♘f7 (the knight is well placed on f7, where it supports the ...e5 break and stops White from placing a knight on e5) 10 ♘a4 ♕d8 = Krasenkov-Piskov, USSR 1989. Black is planning the ...e5 advance.

4...dxe4

It is probably correct to capture this way, so as to keep the f-file closed.

5 f3 ♘f6!?

This is probably Black's best plan: he reaches a form of Staunton Gambit, albeit one where he has already played ...c6. Another option might just about be playable: 5...♕b6 6 ♕d2 ♕xb2 7 ♖b1 e3!? (7...♕a3?! 8 fxe4 fxe4 9 ♗c4 ♘f6 10 ♘ge2 ♘bd7 11 0-0 ♘b6 12 ♗b3 ♗g4 13 h3 ♗d7 14 ♘f4 gave White good compensation in the game Hauchard-Bjørntoft, Kecskemet 1991) 8 ♕xe3 and now:

a) 8...♕a3? 9 ♗c4 h6 10 ♗f4 ♘f6 11 ♘ge2 ♘bd7 and now the unnatural 12 ♔f2?! (Poluliakhov-Glek, USSR Cht (Podolsk) 1990) 12...g5 13 ♗c7 ♘b6 14 ♗b3 ♕a5 gives White compensation for the pawn but nothing crystal clear. Instead, the simple 12 0-0 gives White a big initiative for the pawn.

b) 8...♕xc2! is critical. White has some compensation, but maybe not enough. Poluliakhov gave 9 ♖c1 ♕b2 10 ♘b5 as good for White, but this is easily parried by 10...♕b4+ 11 ♔f2 ♘a6.

6 fxe4 fxe4 7 ♗c4

This is the only way to keep the initiative flowing. 7 ♗xf6 allows Black easy equality: 7...exf6 8 ♘xe4 ♗e6 = (8...♕d5!? is also interesting).

7...♗f5

Black's other sensible option is 7...♗g4 8 ♕d2 ♘bd7 9 h3, and now:

a) 9...♘b6 is also OK for Black: 10 ♗b3 ♗h5 11 ♘ge2 h6 and now, rather than 12 ♗e3?! ♘bd5 ∓ 13 ♗g3 ♗g6 14 ♘ce2 ♘xe3 15 ♕xe3 ♘d5, when Black was firmly in charge in Litus-Malaniuk, Katowice 1991, it is time to win back the lost pawn by 12 ♗xf6 exf6 13 ♘xe4 ♗f7 =.

b) 9...♗h5 10 g4 ♗g6 11 0-0-0 e5 12 ♘ge2 ♗e7 13 ♘g3 ♘b6 14 ♗e6 ♘fd5 15 ♗xe7 ♕xe7 16 ♘xd5 cxd5 17 ♘f5 ♗xf5 18 gxf5 exd4 19 ♕xd4 ♖f8 and although Black's king is a little uncomfortable, he remains a pawn up, Timoshchenko-*Fritz*, Jena 1996.

8 ♘ge2 ♕a5 *(D)*

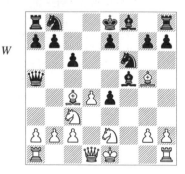

This is a good move, defending the f5-bishop and getting ready to castle queenside.

9 ♕d2 ♘bd7 10 0-0-0 b5 11 ♗b3 b4 12 ♘a4 0-0-0 13 ♖hf1 ♗g4

∓ A.Alonso-U.Rodriguez, Asturia 1997.

10 White Avoids d4 – the English Set-Up

1 c4 f5 2 ♘c3 ♘f6 3 g3 c6 4 ♗g2 ♗e7
5 d3 0-0 (D)

W

White's Strategy

With 5 d3 White does not try to prevent Black from playing ...e5 but plays around it, which can be done in two different ways:

1) White strikes out with e4. As we have seen in many lines in the Classical Dutch, White often never manages to play e4, but with a pawn on d3 Black cannot stop White from playing this break.

2) White doesn't take any immediate action in the centre but instead advances on the queenside. This usually involves throwing the b-pawn up the board, with such moves as ♖b1, a3, b4 and b5.

Black's Strategy

Black's plan is generally the same against both of White's methods of play. The basic strategy should run something along the following lines:

1) Play the ...e5 advance. In some cases it is worth waiting a while before playing this, so as to develop the dark-squared bishop outside the pawn-structure. This is especially true when White plays in the centre with e4.

2) Develop the b8-knight to c6. This is more effective for Black now since he does not have to worry about White playing d5. If White advances the b-pawn, the knight should normally retreat to d8 where it can join in the kingside attack via the route f7-g5. This tends to be more effective for Black when he has already played ...g5 and ...g4.

3) Manoeuvre the queen to h5 via e8, so as to step up the pressure against White's kingside.

4) Gain space on the kingside with g5. This is better when White plays b4-b5 since then Black wants to keep the centre closed.

Black has to be very careful if he decides to play ...c6 since this gives White two dangerous breaks. One is b4-b5, when White will be able to exert pressure against Black's queen-side more rapidly than normal. The other break is c5, intending to gain space on the queenside and to break up Black's central pawn-structure. This wouldn't be so dangerous if Black still had his pawn on c7, since then he could always recapture on d6 with his c-pawn. The following game shows a case when c5 caused considerable problems for Black.

Yurtaev – Moskalenko
Riga 1988

1 ♘f3 f5 2 g3 ♘f6 3 ♗g2 e6 4 0-0 ♗e7 5 c4 0-0 6 ♘c3 c6 7 d3 d6 8 e4 e5 9 c5 *(D)*

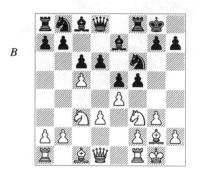

Now Black cannot avoid the exchange of his d6-pawn, which leaves the e5-pawn weak. Here White was able to exploit this to make an immediate central breakthrough.

9...♘a6 10 cxd6 ♗xd6 11 d4 ♘xe4 12 dxe5 ♘xc3 13 bxc3 ♗e7 14 ♘d4 ♔h8 15 ♕e2 ♗c5 16 ♖e1 ♘c7 17 ♘b3

...and White's e-pawn determined the result.

The Theory of the English Set-Up

1 c4 f5 2 ♘c3 ♘f6 3 g3 e6

It is also possible to choose 3...d6 with the idea of playing ...e5 in one move. Personally, I am always pleased when White avoids playing d4. This is due to the fact that Black can play ...e5 at will, when he can expect good play and few real problems for the rest of the game. The lines below show an interesting plan for Black.

4 ♗g2 ♗e7 5 d3

5 ♘f3 is in some ways a more flexible move-order, as White leaves himself the option of playing either d3 or d4 depending on what Black does. However, after 5...0-0 6 0-0 d6 White must play d4 or d3 at some point, leading to familiar positions. For example, 7 d4 transposes to the Ilyin-Zhenevsky System (Chapters 1-3), while 7 d3 reaches Line C of this chapter.

5...0-0

Now White can choose from:
A: 6 e4?!   110
B: 6 e3   113
C: 6 ♘f3   113

The first allows Black an easy game, as he has not yet firmly determined the role of his e7-bishop. White's other main plan here is to leave matters in the centre as they are, and try a pawn-storm on the queenside. This is normally met by kingside and central play by Black.

A)
6 e4?! fxe4 7 dxe4 ♘c6 *(D)*

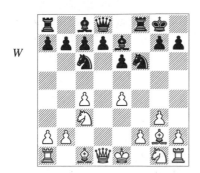

Black's idea is to develop his dark-squared bishop to b4 or c5 and then to continue with ...d6, ...e5, ...♕e8 and ...♕h5. Now White can choose from three moves:

A1: 8 ♘f3   111
A2: 8 h3   111
A3: 8 ♘ge2   112

A1)

8 ♘f3 ♗b4

8...♗c5 is also a good move, and leads to an equal position.

9 e5

After 9 ♕c2 ♗xc3+ 10 bxc3 d6 ∓, with ...e5 coming next, Black is better due to White's weakened c-pawns.

9...♘e4 10 ♗d2 ♗xc3 11 ♗xc3 ♘xc3 12 bxc3 (D)

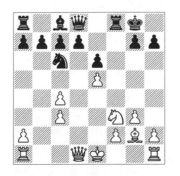

This position is roughly equal. Black's pawn-structure is rock solid compared to White's flimsy mass, but White does have more space. Snape-S.Williams, British Ch (Scarborough) 2001 continued 12...♕e7 13 0-0 ♖b8 (13...♕c5 also looks perfectly natural) 14 ♕e2 b6 15 ♘d4 ♘a5 16 ♘b3 ♗b7 17 f4 ♘c5 18 ♘d4 ♗b7.

A2)

8 h3 (D)

Given that White can still continue ♘ge2, there is no point in Black playing ...♗b4.

8...♗c5

This is the most ambitious move. Black wants to place his bishop outside the pawn-formation of ...d6 and ...e5. However, he can also leave the bishop on e7 and play ...d6 followed by ...e5, when he can be happy with his position.

9 ♘ge2

This is probably White's best. At first sight 9...♗xf2+ looks like a killer blow, but it does not quite work.

The only practical example continued 9 ♘f3 d6 10 0-0 ♕e8 11 ♕e2 ♕g6

♕ and Black's pieces were more actively placed in McNab-S.Williams, Oxford 1998.

9...d6

After 9...♗xf2+!? 10 ♔xf2 ♘xe4++ 11 ♔g1 ♘f2 Black ends up with a material advantage but White's minor pieces are too strong: 12 ♕c2 ♘xh1 13 ♔xh1 e5 14 ♗e4 ± and Black's king is looking very exposed against White's bishops, which dominate the b1-h7 and c1-h6 diagonals.

10 0-0 a6

Black's dark-squared bishop is a useful piece to keep; this move parries ♘a4 since it can now be answered by ...♗a7. Black will have a very active position after the standard manoeuvre ...♕e8-h5 followed by ...e5: every piece is in its ideal position.

11 ♔h2?

Black has the strong reply against this but it is not easy to find a good plan for White. For example, 11 ♗g5 can simply be met by 11...h6 12 ♗xf6 ♕xf6 ♕.

11...♘e5! (D)

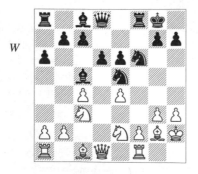

12 b3 ♘eg4+! 13 hxg4 ♘xg4+ 14 ♔g1 ♖xf2! 15 ♖xf2 ♗xf2+ 16 ♔h1

16 ♔f1 does not help either due to 16...♕f6.

16...♗xg3

Black is winning.

A3)

8 ♘ge2 (D)

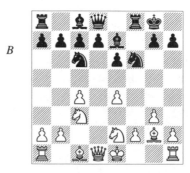

This is White's most natural move, since it allows the f-pawn to advance if needed, and gives extra cover to the c3-knight. However, it also gives Black the option of playing an interesting idea.

8...♘g4!?

8...♗c5 threatens ...♘g4, which gives White no choice but to play 9 h3, transposing to Line A2, where Black is doing fine.

9 ♘f4

This is forced, or else White suffers a disaster on f2.

9...♘ge5

9...♘xf2 is another option but it allows White to obtain a grip on the centre. After 10 ♔xf2 e5 11 ♗e3 exf4 12 gxf4 the position is about equal since White's king is slightly misplaced but he does control the centre.

10 b3

This is the only way to avoid the loss of the c-pawn. For example, 10 ♕e2?! fails to 10...g5 11 ♘d3 ♘xc4.

10...a6!

With the idea of playing ...b5 followed, if White accepts the pawn, by ...♗a6, trapping the white king in the centre.

11 ♗b2

If White tries to castle he can get into trouble: 11 0-0 b5 ∓ 12 cxb5 axb5 13 ♘xb5? ♗a6 and White has to give up the exchange since 14 ♕e2? fails to 14...♘d4 −+.

11...b5 12 cxb5 axb5 13 ♘xb5

Declining the b5-pawn gives Black too much queenside play.

13...♗a6 14 a4 ♗b4+ 15 ♔f1 *(D)*

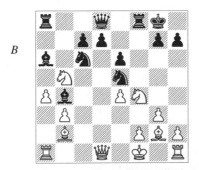

Black has good compensation for the pawn. He always has the option of playing ...♘a7 at some point, regaining the pawn. Play might continue:

15...♕b8

15...♕f6 is another interesting option for Black.

16 ♕e2 ♕b6 17 ♖d1 ♗c5

Black has enough pressure against the white position to compensate for the pawn.

B)

6 e3 *(D)*

This set-up need not worry Black.

6...d5

Normally playing a Stonewall set-up against White's quiet development allows a quick e4, but here White has already played e3, so Black is OK. Black can still continue with the Classical set-up against White's passive plan if he wishes; for example, 6...d6 7 ♘ge2 c6 8 0-0 e5 9 ♖b1 ♗e6 10 f4 ♘bd7 11 b4 ♕c7 12 ♗d2 ♔h8 13 b5 ♘c5 14 ♕c2 e4! 15 d4 ♘d3 = Sinclair-Galligam, Mulcahy 1974.

7 cxd5 exd5 8 ♕b3

If 8 ♘ge2 Black can play 8...c6 with equality.

8...c6 9 e4

This attempt to exploit the fact that Black has played ...d5 doesn't work, which is not surprising considering White has lost a tempo with e3 and e4.

9...♘bd7

The chances are approximately equal.

C)

6 ♘f3! *(D)*

In positions like this the move-order is quite important. This is trickier for Black to deal with than 6 e4.

6...d6! 7 0-0 ♘c6

We shall take a brief look at another plan, since it features some instructive and thematic play: 7...♕e8 8 ♖b1 ♔h8 (a useful waiting move but it is not strictly necessary) 9 b4 ♕h5 10 ♕c2 a6 (it is hard for White to break down Black's queenside with this set-up; note that Black avoids playing ...c6, since this would give White a target to attack with b5) 11 ♗d2 e5 12 b5 ♘bd7 13 a4 ♘g4 14 h3 (Black loses time but he has forced White to weaken his kingside; h3 is now a target for the c8-bishop; another useful feature {for Black} of the pawn being on h3 is that the g5-knight cannot re-route via the h3-square) 14...♘gf6 15 d4 e4 16 ♘g5 ♘b6 17 c5 ♘bd5 18 ♘xd5 ♘xd5 ∓ Miralles-Bricard, Montpellier 1991.

Now (after 7...♘c6) White has two plans:

C1: 8 ♖b1   114
C2: 8 e4   115

C1)

8 ♖b1 (D)

White makes his plan clear: he intends to rush his b-pawn up the board, supported by the c-pawn and the g2-bishop. This plan can potentially create a lot of pressure against Black's queenside.

It is never clear whether the move ...a5 helps or hinders Black. In my opinion it is better to leave the pawn on a7. This is because after the a-pawns are exchanged, both players have the extra option of infiltrating down the a-file. As Black's counterplay is on the kingside, this will only help White. Black's queenside is also harder to break down when he leaves the pawn on a7.

8...♕e8

Manoeuvring the queen over to h5 is natural, since from there it exerts annoying pressure on the white kingside. 8...e5 will usually transpose to 8...♕e8 lines.

9 b4 e5 10 b5 ♘d8

Now A.Vaulin-Shtyrenkov, Katowice 1992 continued 11 a4 ♘e6 12 ♗a3 g5 = (it is hard for White to break down Black's queenside, and it is hard for Black to break down White's kingside) 13 ♘d5 ♘xd5 14 cxd5 ♘g7 15

♕b3 ♗f6 16 ♖fc1 ♕f7 17 ♖c4 g4 18 ♘d2 ♗g5 19 e3 ♘e8 20 ♕c2 b6 21 ♖c1 ♗b7 22 ♕b3 =.

C2)

8 e4 e5 (D)

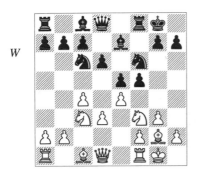

Black has lost a tempo, but this is of little importance as he has achieved the ...e5 push. Black's aim now is either to exchange on e4 at the right moment and play ...♗g4 and ...♘d4 with good piece-play, or to transfer the queen to the kingside via e8 in the hope of forcing checkmate, which is, after all, the aim of the game.

White has now tried three moves, of which only one poses any threat to Black's set-up.

9 h3!

This is Timman's idea. White wants to exchange on f5 and play d4. Other moves:

a) 9 exf5 ♗xf5 10 d4 (if White plays 10 ♘h4 then Black can reply 10...♗g4 =) 10...♗g4! = is fine for Black; e.g., 11 d5 ♘d4.

b) 9 ♘d5 is the most natural continuation, but Black still has an easy game after 9...fxe4! (Black understands the demands of the position: to continue ...♗g4 and ...♘d4, securing good piece-play) 10 dxe4 ♗g4 11 ♕d3 ♘d7 = 12 ♘e1 ♘c5 13 ♕d2 ♘d4 (another idea is 13...a5) 14 f3 ♗h5 15 b4 ♘ce6 16 ♗b2 ♗g5 17 ♕f2 c6 18 ♘e3 (Ehlvest-Makarychev, USSR 1988) and now Black should play 18...♗g6 with a slight advantage.

9...♕e8

This is the most natural plan. White has weakened his kingside with h3, so Black plans to place his queen on the aggressive h5-square. 9...♔h8 was previously played but this makes little sense; Black has to play energetically.

10 exf5

Continuing with Timman's plan. After 10 ♘d5 ♗d8 = Black is solid and has chances to attack with ...♕h5.

10...♗xf5 11 d4 ♕h5 (D)

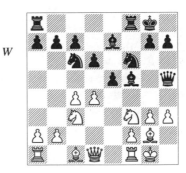

12 ♘h4!

This logical move is yet to be tried in practice. White has to swap the queens off, since otherwise Black's attack will be too strong. Other moves leave White in trouble:

a) 12 g4? ♗xg4 13 hxg4 ♘xg4 offers Black the dream Dutch position!

b) 12 ♘d5? ♗xh3 13 dxe5 and now:

b1) 13...♘g4?! (Black is threatening 14...♗xg2 15 ♔xg2 ♖xf3!) 14 ♘f4 ♖xf4 15 ♗xf4! (15 gxf4?! dxe5 16 ♕d5+ ♔h8 17 fxe5 ♖f8 gave Black a raging attack in Mah-S.Williams, Witley 1999) 15...dxe5 16 ♕d5+ ♔h8 17 ♘xe5 may give White an edge.

b2) 13...♗xg2! 14 ♔xg2 dxe5 gives Black a strong initiative.

c) 12 d5 ♘a5! (forcing matters) 13 ♕a4 (other moves are no better: 13 b3 ♗xh3 14 ♗xh3 ♕xh3 15 ♘g5 ♕f5 16 ♘e6 ♖fc8 ∓ and Black will bring his a5-knight around to c5 by ...b6, ...♘b7 and ...♘c5, swapping off White's annoying e6-knight, when he will stay a pawn up) 13...b6 14 g4? ♗xg4 –+.

12...♗d7!

Other continuations leave Black in trouble.

13 dxe5 dxe5 14 ♘d5 ♕xd1 15 ♖xd1 *(D)*

Capturing Black's c7-bishop doesn't help: 15 ♘xe7+ ♘xe7 16 ♖xd1 ♗c6 and Black equalizes after swapping off White's strong g2-bishop.

15...♘xd5 16 ♗xd5+

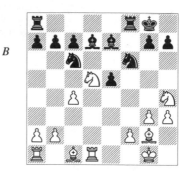

B

16 cxd5 ♘d4 leaves White's knight in trouble.

16...♔h8 17 ♘f3

White cannot allow ...♗xh4, since this would damage his pawn-structure too much.

17...♗c5

This is the safest route to equality. 17...♗xh3?! may allow White to get a slight advantage with 18 ♗xc6 bxc6 19 ♘xe5 ♗c5 20 ♗f4 ±, since Black's two bishops don't make up for his weak queenside pawns.

18 ♔g2 ♖ae8

The game is equal. Black's e-pawn is more of a strength than a weakness due to the possibility of it storming up the e-file.

11 1 ♘f3 Without c4 or d4, Including the Lisitsyn Gambit

The Lisitsyn Gambit (1 ♘f3 f5 2 e4) can be dangerous for Black if he is unprepared, but as with most gambits, if Black has done his homework he has no need to worry. The Lisitsyn Gambit borrows a lot of characteristics from the From Gambit (1 f4 e5 2 fxe5 d6) and has the idea that the knight being on f3 benefits White, because it can quickly take up an aggressive post. It is not clear whether this is true though, since the white knight can also become a target, and White often has to waste time manoeuvring it around to find a safe home.

1 ♘f3 f5

Black can play 1...e6 but he has to be prepared to deal with some off-beat French lines after 2 e4. 1...f5 also gives Black the option of playing ...e5 in one move, which obviously saves a tempo.

White has three independent ways of playing now:

A: 2 d3   117
B: 2 g3   118
C: 2 e4!?   119

A)
    2 d3

This move is harmless if Black responds correctly.

2...d6!

Now that White has shown the intentions of his d-pawn so soon, Black can play ...e5 in one move, without going through the normal process of playing ...e6 first. 2...♘f6? is much less accurate since Black will find it hard to play a quick ...e5.

3 e4 e5 *(D)*

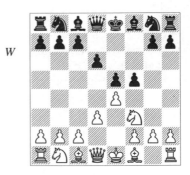

Black has achieved a nice position after just three moves. I think he is comfortably equal.

4 ♘c3 ♘c6

Black does have a more ambitious possibility: 4...♘f6 5 exf5 (if 5 d4, then 5...exd4! 6 ♘xd4 ♘xe4 is equal) 5...♗xf5 6 d4 (if White does nothing then Black will hold the centre with ...c5) and now Black should continue 6...♘bd7 =. Instead 6...e4? 7 ♘h4 ♕d7 8 d5 left White better in Kempter-G.Wall, Germany tt 1999/00.

5 exf5 ♗xf5 6 d4 ♘xd4 7 ♘xd4 exd4 8 ♕xd4 ♘f6 9 ♗d3 ♗xd3 10 ♕xd3 c6 11 0-0 ♗e7 12 ♘e4 ♘xe4

13 ♕xe4 0-0 14 c4 ♗f6 15 ♗e3 d5
½-½ Romanishin-Malaniuk, Tallinn 1987.

B)

2 g3

Black has a couple of equally viable ways to play against this. One idea is to play ...d6 and ...e5 as soon as possible. In that case Black normally has to be willing to meet d4 with ...e4. Here I shall focus on another method that is more in tune with the Classical Dutch.

2...♘f6

Black can also play ...e6 and wait to see how White develops, but this will normally come to the same thing.

3 ♗g2 e6 4 0-0 ♗e7 5 d3

After this move Black's knight will always be safe on c6, as it can't get hit by the white advance d4 and d5.

5...0-0 6 ♘bd2

After 6 ♘c3 it seems that Black has two decent moves:

a) 6...♗b4!? is an interesting idea which has yet to be tried. Black gets ready to play ...d6 and ...e5, with his bishop placed on a more active square. On b4 the bishop also parries the e4 advance. Play might continue 7 ♗d2 (to avoid getting doubled c-pawns)

7...d6 8 a3 and now Black can either play 8...♗xc3 9 ♗xc3 e5 = or the more adventurous 8...♗a5 9 b4 ♗b6 10 ♘a4 e5 =.

b) 6...d6 7 e4 e5 8 exf5 ♗xf5 9 ♘h4 ♗g4 10 f3 ♗c8 = (Black has triumphed in the opening battle) 11 f4 ♘c6 12 fxe5 dxe5 13 h3 ♘d4, Lputian-Bareev, USSR Ch (Kiev) 1986.

6...♘c6 7 e4 fxe4 8 dxe4 ♕e8

Black can always play ...d6 and ...e5, but this way Black intends to develop his dark-squared bishop outside his pawn-chain.

9 e5 ♘g4 10 ♘c4

Other moves are no better. 10 ♖e1?! ♕h5 ∓ leaves White's kingside and e5-pawn subject to attack.

10...♖b8!

Moving the rook off the h1-a8 diagonal and preparing to bring it to a more active square.

11 ♗f4 b5 *(D)*

W

Black has equalized.

12 ♘e3 ♘xe3 13 ♗xe3 b4

Black plans to move his rook to b5, where it increases the pressure on e5.

14 ♖e1 a5

Also interesting is 14...♖b5!?.

15 c4 bxc3 16 bxc3 ♕g6 17 a4 h6 18 ♖a2 ♕g4 19 ♕e2 ♕h5 20 ♕d1 ♕g4

Dorfman-Roos, France 1993 eventually ended in a draw from this position.

C)

2 e4!? *(D)*

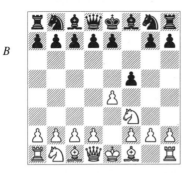

This is called the Lisitsyn Gambit (or the Pirc-Lisitsyn Gambit), and is a dangerous weapon if Black does not know what he is doing. However, if Black returns the pawn at the correct time he can expect an easy game.

2...fxe4

White also has to be prepared for the Latvian Gambit, to which Black can transpose with 2...e5, although I don't recommend this.

3 ♘g5

The Lisitsyn Gambit borrows its characteristics from the From Gambit (1 f4 e5 2 fxe5 d6). White's idea is to play d3, and if Black captures the pawn then White can develop a massive attack with his knight on g5 and bishop on d3. Therefore it is never a good idea for Black to capture on d3.

3...♘c6!?

This rarely played continuation is Black's simplest route to equality. The idea is to avoid blocking the d8-h4 diagonal (which happens after ...♘f6), so Black can play ...♗e7 at some point, kicking back White's knight.

4 d3 e3! *(D)*

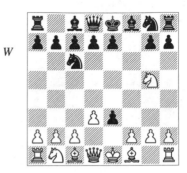

This is a good point to return the pawn. Black can take the centre and stop White's light-squared bishop taking up its ideal place on d3.

5 ♗xe3 e5

Play has transposed to a line which White can get after 3...e5, but playing 3...♘c6 gives White fewer options. White has a number of options here:

C1: 6 ♗e2   120
C2: 6 c4   120
C3: 6 d4!?   120
C4: 6 g3   121

Or:

a) 6 f4 exf4 7 ♗xf4 ♕f6 8 ♕c1 d5 9 ♘c3? (9 ♗e2 is better but Black has no problems after 9...♗c5 =) 9...♗b4 10 ♗d2 ♗c5 ∓ and Black eventually won in Levit-A.Zaitsev, USSR Ch (Leningrad) 1962.

b) 6 ♕h5+ g6 7 ♕f3 ♕f6 (the exchange of queens would favour Black due to his strong centre in the middlegame) 8 ♕g3 ♘ge7 9 ♘c3 h6 10 ♘ge4 ♕f7 11 ♘b5 ♘f5 12 ♕f3 d5 ∓ 13 ♘f6+?! ♕xf6 14 ♘xc7+ ♔d8 15 ♘xa8 e4 16 dxe4 ♕xb2 17 ♕d1? ♘xe3 18 fxe3 ♕c3+ 19 ♔f2 ♗c5 0-1 Robatsch-Larsen, Moscow OL 1956.

C1)
6 ♗e2 *(D)*

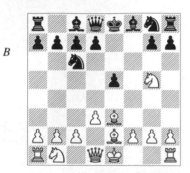

6...♗e7!

Black doesn't want to weaken himself by playing ...h6, so instead kicks White's knight back and develops a piece.

7 ♘f3

Other moves:

a) 7 f4? exf4! 8 ♗h5+ g6 9 ♘xh7 ♘e5! −+.

b) 7 ♗h5+? g6 8 ♘xh7 ♔f7! 9 ♕f3+ ♔g7 and White faces the loss of a piece.

c) After 7 h4 ♘f6 8 ♗h5+ g6 9 ♗f3 h6 10 ♘e4 d5 Black's centre gives him a slight advantage.

7...♘f6 8 d4 exd4 9 ♘xd4 0-0 10 0-0 ♘xd4 11 ♗xd4 d5

= Zude-Lutz, German Ch (Gladenbach) 1997.

C2)
6 c4

White stakes a claim on the centre and temporarily stops Black's plan of playing ...d5. However, this is hardly something Black need fear.

6...♘f6 7 ♘c3 ♗b4! *(D)*

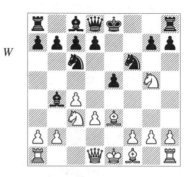

Black still insists on playing ...d5!

8 ♗e2 d5 9 cxd5 ♘xd5 10 ♘ge4 0-0 11 0-0 ♘f4 12 ♗g4 ♗xg4 13 ♕xg4 ♗xc3 14 ♘xc3 ♕xd3

∓ Pilaj-E.Berg, Oropesa del Mar U-18 Wch 1999.

C3)
6 d4!? *(D)*

White resorts to very direct measures. Black must now play some accurate moves, but after the smoke has cleared he should hold a nice advantage.

6...exd4 7 ♗d3

The big threat is 8 ♕h5+.

7...♘f6

I could not find an immediate win following 7...dxe3?! but White has a

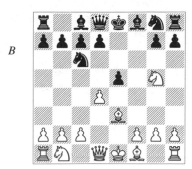

massive attack while Black has only one piece developed, so it is probably best to give it a miss.

8 ♗f4 ♗b4+ 9 c3 ♕e7+ 10 ♔d2!

This is White's only chance to mix things up, but his king may suffer as much as Black's.

10...dxc3+ 11 bxc3 ♗d6!

Other moves are bad. After 11...0-0? 12 ♕b3+ d5 13 cxb4 White obtained an extra piece in W.Richter-Hasse, corr. 1975.

12 ♗g3

Black's king is safe enough after 12 ♗xd6 ♕xd6 13 ♖e1+ ♘e7 ∓.

12...♘d8!

Black wants to block the e-file with ...♘e6 and then castle. 12...♗xg3?! was played in Halmeenmaki-Yrjölä, Helsinki 1999, but it seems suspect to open the h-file if Black can avoid doing so.

13 ♖e1 ♘e6 14 f4 0-0 15 f5 ♗xg3 16 hxg3 ♕c5! *(D)*

Black's queen does a good job hitting the g5-knight.

17 ♕b3 ♔h8 18 ♘xh7

Or 18 ♘xe6 dxe6 19 fxe6 ∓.

18...♘xh7 19 fxe6 dxe6 20 ♖h1 ♕g5+

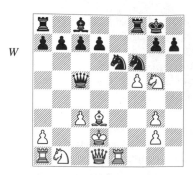

Black has a large advantage. White's king is in mortal danger while Black can play ...g6 if needed.

C4)

6 g3

This is White's safest and probably best move. The idea is to control the d5-square after ♗g2, c4 and ♘c3.

6...♗e7 *(D)*

The alternative 6...♘f6 is also approximately equal.

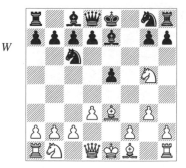

7 ♗g2!

This logical move is yet to be played in practice. Guarding or retreating the white knight is a sign of failure:

a) 7 h4?! (there is no real need for this) 7...♘f6 8 ♗g2 d5 9 d4 ♗g4 10

♕d2 h6 11 ♘f3 ∓ M.Diaz-Friot, French Cht 2000.

b) 7 ♗h3 d5 8 ♘e6 ♗xe6 9 ♗xe6 ♘f6 is equal. Black will continue with ...♕d6 and ...0-0, when his strong centre makes up for White's bishop-pair.

c) 7 ♘e4 d5 only helps Black.

7...d5

7...♗xg5?! concedes the bishop-pair a bit too readily: 8 ♕h5+ g6 9 ♕xg5 ±. White is a bit better due to his bishop-pair and control over the d5-square.

8 0-0

8 c4? is a bit premature since Black can stop White castling with 8...♗b4+! 9 ♔e2 (or 9 ♔f1 dxc4 10 ♗e4 ♘f6 ∓) 9...♘ge7.

8...♗f5! *(D)*

This move continues to restrain the c4 advance. The idea is to keep ...♗xg5 as a threat, while Black may also wish to castle queenside. Also, ...♘h6 is now an idea; previously it would have

failed to ♕h5+, but this can now be met by ...♗g6.

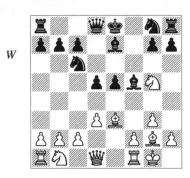

9 f4

Not 9 c4? d4 10 ♗d2 ♗xg5 11 ♕h5+ g6 12 ♕xg5 ♕xg5 13 ♗xg5 h6 14 ♗d2 ♗xd3 ∓.

9...♗xg5 10 fxg5 ♘ge7

The position is about equal. Black holds a nice centre and will shortly get his king to safety, but White has the bishop-pair.

12 Other Lines

The Dutch is playable against most of White's first moves (two cases in which I wouldn't recommended playing it would be against 1 e4 and 1 g4, for obvious reasons!). In this chapter I will briefly examine using the Dutch against irregular openings.

Other moves:

a) 1 c3 f5 2 ♕c2 (I would be very surprised ever to come across this plan in tournament chess, or any kind of chess for that matter, but if White is going to play 1 c3 then I guess 2 ♕c2 is the 'natural' reply to 1...f5) 2...e6 (Black can also play 2...d6 or 2...d5, when he has already equalized due to his strong centre; if he wants to join the fun and go a bit mental himself then 2...♘c6 meeting 3 ♕xf5 with 3...d5 is a possibility) 3 d3 ♘f6 4 g3 ♘c6 5 ♗g2 b6 6 ♘f3 ♗b7 7 ♘bd2 ♗e7 8 a4 (dynamic play from White, pushing a pawn past the third rank) 8...0-0 9 b4 a6 10 0-0 ♕e8 switching the queen over to join a kingside attack, Nguyen Huu-Rue, St Quentin 1999.

b) 1 b4 f5 2 ♗b2 ♘f6 and then:

b1) 3 e3 e6 4 b5 ♗e7 5 ♘f3 0-0 6 c4 d6 7 ♗e2 e5 8 d4 e4 9 ♘fd2 ♕e8 10 ♘c3 ♕g6 11 g3 = Teichmann-Bhend, Berne 1991.

b2) 3 ♗xf6 exf6 4 a3 a5 5 b5 f4!? 6 ♘h3 ♗d6 7 ♘c3 ♕e7 8 g3 fxg3 9 hxg3 c6 10 a4 ♗e5 11 ♘f4 ♗xf4 12 gxf4 d5 13 d4 ♗f5 = Bulcourf-Bianchi, Argentine Ch (San Martin) 1987.

A)

1 b3

Black has to be careful with the move-order here.

1...f5 2 ♗b2 ♘f6

2...e6? is a mistake due to 3 e4! fxe4 4 ♕h5+ ♔e7 (not 4...g6? 5 ♕e5 +−), when Black's king is rather exposed.

3 ♗xf6 exf6 (D)

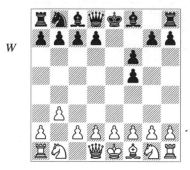

I think Black can expect equality here.

4 e3 d5 5 d4 ♗d6

The immediate 5...c5 is probably better.

6 g3 c5 7 ♘e2 ♘c6 8 c3 cxd4 9 cxd4

9 exd4 f4!?.

9...♕a5+ 10 ♘d2 ♗a3

Black is slightly better, G.Welling-Teichmann, Melbourne 2000.

B)

1 d3

This is a very rare move indeed. Black should consider playing the natural 1...e5, when he has already equalized, but we shall take a look at what happens if Black sticks to the pure Dutch approach.

1...f5 2 e4

Other moves will either lead back to lines covered in previous chapters or are bad for White. For example, 2 c4 ♘f6 gives Black a very pleasant position, as White's normal break d4 will not be as effective because the pawn has already wasted time moving to d3.

2...d6 3 exf5 ♗xf5 4 g4 ♗d7 5 ♗g2 ♘c6 6 ♘c3 e5 7 h3 ♘ge7 8 ♗g5 ♗e6 9 ♘ge2 h6 10 ♗h4 g5 11 ♗g3 ♗g7 12 ♕d2 ♕d7

Husari-Hoang Thanh Tran, Budapest 2001.

C)

1 g3 f5

Play will normally transpose to one of lines already examined within this book, but White does have some other, rather dubious options.

2 ♗g2

With 2 e4?! White is trying to reach a From Gambit (1 f4 e5) with a pawn on g3 instead of g2. However, it is doubtful whether this extra move gives

White any benefits. 2...fxe4 3 d3 ♘f6 (there is also nothing wrong with accepting the gambit by 3...exd3 4 ♗xd3 ♘f6, when White's best move might be 5 g4, reaching a line from the From Gambit) 4 dxe4 e5 5 ♗c4 ♗c5 = (the move g3 has weakened White's kingside) 6 ♘f3 b5!? (a nice idea, distracting the white bishop to speed Black's development) 7 ♗xb5 0-0 8 ♘xe5 ♕e7 9 ♘f3 ♘xe4 10 0-0 (White's position looks ropy) 10...♗b7 11 ♗e2 ♕f7 12 ♗f4 ♕f5 13 b4 ♗b6 (13...♗xb4 is also OK for Black) 14 c4 ♘xf2 15 ♖xf2 ♗xf2+ 16 ♔xf2 g5 17 ♗xc7 g4 leaves White's pieces and king badly placed, so Black has the advantage, Cerrajeria-Ansola, Zaragoza 1998.

2...♘f6 3 d3 *(D)*

White plans e4, but after the exchange ...fxe4, dxe4, the g2-bishop will be seriously worried about what the future holds. The bishop really belongs on c4 in this type of position; on g2 its range is very limited due to the white pawn being on e4.

3...e5

Now that White has played d3, Black does not have to worry so much about d4, which can be an irritating response to ...e5.

4 e4

4 c4 is liable to leave Black a tempo up on Chapter 10, while 4 d4!? may be White's best other option.

4...fxe4! 5 dxe4

The position has similarities with Line A of Chapter 10, but here Black has not wasted time moving his bishop to e7.

5...♗c5

Black is already a bit better.

6 ♘c3

6 ♘e2?! is asking for it: 6...♘g4 7 f3 ♗f2+ (7...♕f6 is interesting) 8 ♔f1 ♖f8?! (it is time for Black to play 8...♗e3, when he has an advantage due to White's misplaced king) 9 ♕d3 (a better attempt is 9 fxg4, which looks risky but is good for White) 9...♗b6 10 ♘bc3 ♘f2 11 ♕d5 d6 12 ♖g1 ♘g4 13 ♖h1 ♘c6 14 ♘d1 ♕e7 15 ♔e1 ♘f6 16 ♕b5 ♗d7 and Black has gained the advantage, Bruns-Krizsany, Finkenstein 1998.

6...0-0 7 ♘f3 d6 8 0-0 a6 9 ♕d3 ♔h8 10 ♗g5 ♗e6 11 ♘h4 ♘bd7 12 ♘d5 c6 13 ♘xf6 ♘xf6 14 ♗e3 ♕a5 15 b3 d5!

Black has a slight advantage, Todorčević-Barlov, Yugoslav Ch (Pljevlja) 1989.

D)

1 ♘c3

It is risky to play the Dutch against this move since White can break in the centre with e4 straight away, after which Black's king is looking a bit bare.

1...f5 2 e4

Other moves are not as testing or have already been examined earlier in the book. For example, 2 d4 transposes to Line C of Chapter 9.

2...fxe4 *(D)*

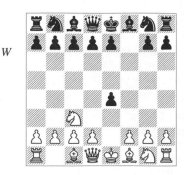

3 d3

3 ♘xe4 g6 and now 4 d4 transposes to a sideline of the Staunton Gambit that is considered OK for Black: 4...d5 5 ♘g5 (5 ♘g3 ♗g7 6 h4 ♘c6 7 ♗b5 ♕d6 =) 5...♗g7 6 ♗d3 ♕d6 7 f4 ♘c6 8 c3 is unclear. A more interesting idea is 4 h4!? intending 5 h5, softening up Black's kingside.

3...♘f6

There are two alternatives, of which one may be OK for Black:

a) 3...exd3?! is paved with danger as White gets to play a From Gambit with an extra tempo. The standard From Gambit is tricky enough anyway, but here Black will be doing well to survive. Here is a good example of what can happen to Black's position: 4 ♗xd3 ♘f6 5 g4 g6 6 g5 ♘h5 7 ♘e4 (making use of the extra tempo, but 7 ♘ge2 might be better) 7...d5 8 ♘g3 ♘xg3 9 hxg3 ♗g7? (9...♕d6! is far more resilient; then White merely has good compensation) 10 ♖xh7! 0-0? 11 ♗xg6 ♕d6 12 ♕h5 ♕e6+ 13 ♗e3 1-0 Rost-Rosher, corr. 1989.

b) 3...e3 is probably the safest way to play: 4 ♗xe3 ♘f6 5 ♘f3 (if 5 g4 then 5...d5 looks fine for Black) 5...e6 6 d4 (White may hold a small edge here due to his space advantage) 6...c6 (this looks a bit odd; developing with 6...♘c6 may be better) 7 ♗d3 ♘a6 8 a3 ♗e7 9 ♘g5 0-0 10 h4 ♘c7 11 ♘ce4 ♘ce8 12 g4? (12 ♘g3) 12...d5 13 ♘g3 ♕c7 14 ♘h3 e5 15 g5 ♘g4 ∓ Donka-Mozes, Hungarian Cht 1992.

4 dxe4

4 g4 may prove more troublesome for Black: 4...e6 5 dxe4 ♗b4 (given that the counterplay against e4 doesn't work, Black should seek an improvement here or on the previous move) 6 g5 ♘g8 (White's initiative now develops unhindered, but after 6...♘xe4 7 ♕d4 ♗xc3+ 8 bxc3 ♘xg5 9 ♕xg7 ♘f7 10 ♗e2 ♕h4 11 ♘f3 ♕h5 12

♖g1 White's attack is decisive) 7 ♗g2 ♘c6 8 a3 ♗xc3+ 9 bxc3 ♘ge7 10 ♕h5+ ♘g6 11 f4 d6 and White has an advantage due to the possibility of creating an attack against the black king, Neshtukov-Bogachev, Novokuznetsk 1997.

4...e5 5 ♘f3 ♗b4 6 ♗c4 ♕e7 7 0-0 ♗xc3 8 bxc3 d6 (D)

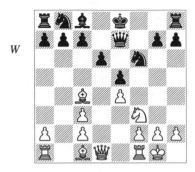

The position is equal, Zwinkels-Heymann, Bethune 2001. Black will be able to play ...♗e6 and then castle, when he has nothing to worry about.

Index of Variations

Chapter Guide

1: The Ilyin-Zhenevsky System with 7...a5

2: The Ilyin-Zhenevsky System with 7...♕e8

3: The Ilyin-Zhenevsky System with 7...♘e4!